Charlotte Miller was born in The Netherlands, immigrating to Canada in 1951 with her family. She and her husband George live in Scarborough. As retirees, they enjoy gardening and trips along the back roads searching for classic Ontario style architecture but most of all they enjoy talking to anyone who loves cats as much as they do!

I dedicate my first book to the love of my life, my husband George, whose dogged patience continually corrected my "faultless" efforts…his chortles were all the encouragement I needed. I am thankful to the friends, including the one who is terrified of cats and others, who reviewed these stories and offered their comments, such as, "It's purrfect!"

Charlotte Miller

SCARBOROUGH TALES: TALES: SHORT & LONG

AUSTIN MACAULEY
PUBLISHERS LTD.

A CIP catalogue record for this title is available from the British Library.

ISBN 9781784555979 (Paperback)
ISBN 9781784555986 (Hardback)
ISBN 9781784555993 (E-Book)

www.austinmacauley.com

First Published (2016)
Austin Macauley Publishers Ltd.
25 Canada Square
Canary Wharf
London
E14 5LQ

In many stories the names of people, places, and pets have been changed to preserve their privacy.

Contents

Prologue

I love cats,
without reservation.
Aside from caring for their needs,
I love hearing, talking and reading about them.
A few have crossed my path;
sixteen tales all told.

Spouse George has
encouraged the writing of my stories and
upon reading them, I've heard him chuckle softly.
Cat lovers know, and others will
realize, that each cat is
unique.

Dignified or clowns:
affectionate, gluttonous or timid,
trusting or, having seen it all, skeptical,
lazybones, hunters, and lovers;
endless qualities
like us.

Cats do not love me.
A warm shelter and larder am I.
A groomer; perhaps a friend and at their whim
perhaps entreated or cajoled.
I have no illusions;
I still love cats.

Costas

Feline Costas has pale amber eyes set in glossy short-haired fur that is black as midnight on a moonless night. With only the slightest encouragement, he will approach to greet a friendly human; flop on the ground, expose his tummy expecting a caress and purr loudly. The flip-side to that friendliness is his ferocity towards other male cats in his territory. Immediately after the heat of a battle, do not expect to encounter a purring pussycat for he is still totally focussed upon his foe. An inveterate fighter in spite of his disability; for Costas, you should know, has only three legs.

Several years ago he almost lost his life in a car accident. So badly mangled was his right hind leg that the veterinarian suggested Costas be put to sleep. Such a loss was unthinkable for the Greek owner's young son who was devastated and would not accept life without Costas. The young son personally pleaded with the veterinarian to please, please save their black cat and so, the right hind leg was amputated. His grievous wound healed and with that blasé attitude of all animals, Costas continued with the business of living. On three legs, he hobbles around far and wide as though his impediment is non-existent. Costas knows that nature neither accepts nor forgives weakness. Whether one has all four or fewer legs, one's territory must be protected. Borders must be inspected, defined and marked on a daily basis and intruders must be ruthlessly expelled! Yet for tripodal Costas each encounter is physically overwhelming as evidenced by the scabs and scars covering his body. Nevertheless, he remains undeterred. Small of stature yet great in spirit, an indomitable Costas meets each challenge. Even in defeat this tripod is, in my opinion, always victorious. Here's to Greek Costas: a warrior extraordinaire worthy of his Mount Olympus ancestors!

Nigel

Nigel is a good-natured, mature resident cat at a pet food store in the village of Hawthorne. It's his honour to be the store's mascot fulfilling several duties. First and foremost, he is the store's official greeter and positions himself purposefully, near the front entrance. Secondly; Nigel is the store's "model", his beautiful amber eyes capturing your attention from several advertising posters hung throughout the store. Last but not least, a minor but essential duty is to keep pesky field mice away from the store's huge supply of dry food. He performs his duties exceptionally well; Nigel is gainfully employed!

I specifically refer to Nigel as "mature" because there are usually many immature kittens scurrying hither and thither around the premises as well. He patiently accommodates all playful youngsters, allowing them to romp around and nip any part of his body. Though clients are fascinated by these kittens, they, in turn, are not at all interested in "greeting" their new admirers. Instead, Nigel compensates for the kittens' lack of manners by dutifully greeting one and all visitors and for that purpose, as stated earlier, he remains close to the front door.

When a prospective client enters, Nigel begins his routine. He pads softly to the middle of the narrow aisle and sits in front of the visitor, looks up, blinks convivially and begins to purr loudly. Such a charming greeting generates the anticipated human response of endearing words accompanied by soft stroking. When Nigel's greeting is complete, he steps aside allowing the client to do their shopping. As duty is done, Nigel knows his visitor was graciously welcomed and sits awaiting his next client.

The explanation for his "model" quality is easily explained. His large round eyes are a deep, warm, tawny colour nestled in charcoal grey fur. It's no wonder Nigel's image is used to advertise this store's product, for one look at his eyes and you will find yourself mesmerized by two liquid pools of luscious amber. Nigel belongs to the British Shorthair breed but apparently due to a recessive long-haired gene, his charcoal fur is long. As a British Shorthair, he might be an enigma but as a "model", Nigel is unique!

There is one more duty that is allotted to Nigel by store management; one that he clearly relishes above all others. He is the store's official taste tester, a duty that Nigel accepts as a labour of love. Only if and when a new type or flavour of food meets with Nigel's personal approval, it will appear on the store's shelving. His discerning taste-buds and dedication to the selection of fine feline cuisine are accepted by store management with total confidence.

All resident felines, young or mature, have the run of the store; all day, every day. Naturally, there is a cornucopia of nutritious kitten food available for energetic growing youngsters. However, since the arrival of the last litter of kittens, Nigel has availed himself overzealously of the kittens' rich, high protein buffet; compared to their diet, his tastes bland. As a consequence, the kittens have grown tremendously, as they should, but so has mature Nigel, who should not! He has grown to rotund proportions; a round butterball, many pounds beyond his ideal weight of twelve pounds. One would conclude that Nigel has been a tad too gainfully employed!

Personally, I like cats a shade on the chubby side because they are then so deliciously cuddly but rotund like an over-ripe watermelon...no! It's clear that Nigel's overindulgence at the midnight buffet has to be curtailed. His owner is alarmed and trying to interest him in diet food, but for anyone who has ever tried to reduce a cat's intake of food, they will know that it is a thankless task. Perhaps a barricade preventing Nigel's access to the kittens' food bowls, will aid in achieving his former svelte form.

His current size prevents him from grooming himself and due to sensitive skin, he rejects attempts to being groomed either with a special comb or soft brush. The solution to his matted long fur was a summer shave. With a shorn coat, Nigel resembles the British Shorthair breed of his ancestors, but to my regret and for the time being, he no longer is the glorious long-haired Nigel I knew.

Sadly, his current size has made him lethargic and he no longer wanders over to greet visitors. The effort is too exhausting. Instead, a "Kitty Hammock" has been positioned near the front entrance and Nigel is doing a fine job demonstrating for hours at a stretch, the many relaxing postures possible in this new contraption, to customers pausing to greet him. Regardless of his size, for me "Star Nigel" will remain an adorable, lovable feline and the store's proud professional feline!

PS…During a visit to the store in January 2009, we learned that Nigel had "retired" to a well-deserved life of leisure with his "nana". Apparently, Nigel, at the grand age of twelve, had reached that stage where he could no longer repel unruly behaviour directed towards him by visiting dogs. Canine harassment had become overwhelming for our mascot and store management did "the right thing". Customers, sorely missing his welcome presence, gather regularly to reminisce about amber-eyed Nigel with the consensus that he was a great mascot. Quite a legacy to leave behind, wouldn't you agree?

Chicken

In the fall of 1989, while we lived on Glynnhoven Road, a classic tabby cat named "Chicken" moved in next door. I was delighted at the prospect of having a "furry" neighbour because I hoped that befriending this feline would be a practical solution to not having a pet cat of our own. Unfortunately for me, Chicken was not in the least interested in my friendly overtures; all my attempts were discouraged by hissing which was generally followed by a pronounced spitting or even a distinct growl. "Pity" I thought, but I am not easily discouraged and realized that great patience was required.

Her unusual name apparently originated from the favourite food of the owner's young children. Potentially, with green eyes and classic tabby markings, she might have been a pretty little cat though too thin for my liking. Her short-haired fur was not vibrant as it lacked the sheen of a healthy coat and on each of her hind legs, bald spots were noticeable. Her whiskers were sparse and her tail was a sad, skimpy looking appendage. Although she was a "pet", we wondered if perhaps she was responsible for hunting her own food. No matter what the season, Chicken seemed to be outdoors more often than not; whether by choice or not, we do not know.

In the early spring of 1990, it became apparent that she was pregnant; her tummy bulging a little more each week. As her size increased, the condition of her fur became even sadder looking. I felt it was time to give her some help. From one of George's fishing trips, we still had a very good supply of smelts in our freezer. Having already had our fill of smelts for this year, we could not stomach another and so a good supply remained in our freezer. Surely a skinny pregnant cat would be happy to have some fish?

17

In the microwave we thawed out and heated several smelts, one of which we took outside to the driveway within Chicken's sight. We then retreated and waited, watching from around the corner. It did not take her very long to approach and within a few seconds, the smelt was gone. We brought out another. That one too, was gone quickly. We brought out one more and yet another. Seven smelts later Chicken finally had her fill. We could not believe how much she had just consumed but then she was eating for who knows how many!

It wasn't long before our supply of smelts had been put to good use and Chicken sat waiting in our driveway to be fed. She no longer hissed or spat but was still cautious and would not let us touch her. Feeding her became a regular habit; in the morning before we left for work and in the evening upon returning home from work. The results of regular feeding soon became obvious. The bald spots on her hind legs were gone, replaced by a new growth of fur and her whiskers grew back thick and long. There must have been at least one long-hair gene in her make-up because she became a lovely semi long-haired tabby. Her tail was now a long-haired plume, proudly held high.

As the weather was still cold, I progressively moved the food bowl closer to our back door; the plan being to feed her inside on the back landing until the warmer months and then outside again. This plan actually progressed faster than I had anticipated. Eating for herself plus however many were developing in her tummy, she was so hungry that within a few days she cautiously came inside to the back landing, quickly devouring greater quantities of food.

Her initial caution soon gave way and if her food wasn't ready, she came up the stairs, from the landing, and into the kitchen where Dickens' (our own newly adopted cat) food bowl was located. Dickens, who had never been hungry in his life, always approached his food bowl with calm dignity. Occasionally, Chicken reached Dicken's food bowl first and that resulted in a short but decisive battle between the two felines. Wisely, pregnant Chicken retreated. By then I had her food bowl ready and she would eagerly follow me down the few stairs to the back door landing; her own designated private eating spot.

Now, I must admit to an ulterior motive. I knew if Chicken accepted food from us then she would likely bring her kittens to us once they were weaned. I have always wanted, but never had the opportunity, to observe a mother cat with kittens. This, at long last, might be my chance. Weeks went by and at last when Chicken was unbelievably huge, she did not come for her regular feeding. Inquiries from my neighbour confirmed that Chicken had given birth to a litter of four healthy kittens in a box behind their couch in their living room. My neighbour also told me that several weeks after the birth, Chicken deposited a "fresh kill" outside the birth-box to entice her kittens. Good motherly instincts, but her owners were not too pleased to find a dead bird in their living room, fresh or not!

About a month after the birth, we saw the little kittens outside. Wobbly at first and then as they grew in strength and co-ordination, we watched their delightful playful antics. As mentioned earlier, there were four kittens; a classic spotted tabby, a striped tabby, one almost completely black and another striped tabby with a white chin, tummy, legs and feet. Chicken was a wonderful mother, carefully supervising all their antics and constantly calling advice to them. As playful youngsters though, they paid not the slightest attention to their mother.

As I had hoped, Chicken eventually brought her kittens to us for meal. It was now much warmer so that they were fed outside in our backyard. There they were, Mother and four little ones, encircling a substantial plate of food. The little ones stepped, or sat, right in their food as they ate. No matter, Mother would clean them later and perhaps nurse them at the same time. It was an adorable sight and my lifelong wish fulfilled: I was in heaven!

As Chicken got to know us better, she relaxed just a little in our presence but only to the point where she occasionally allowed us to pet her. Once, just after she had eaten, George could not resist and picked her up onto his lap; she remained perhaps two seconds before jumping off and hissing at him. No, she would not be our lap-cat. Overall, she remained wary with us although she did not seem to mind us playing with her kittens. We wondered what made her so wary and if she was anyone's lap-cat.

Of course, the kittens got quite used to our presence so that we could pet them, pick them up and play with them. We often sat outside just to watch all their antics. At one time a kitten was playing next to Dickens when it tumbled and rolled into him. The kitten immediately stood up, turned around and hissed at Dickens who, having had limited interaction with other cats, looked perplexed and likely wondered what it all meant. Thankfully, he did not retaliate because this kitten was barely the size of Dickens' head. What a brave little soul!

As the kittens grew, so did their appetites and one evening when their dinner was late, George's son Jeremy, got the surprise of his life. Hearing something at the front door, he looked through the peep-hole to see who was calling at dinnertime. In fish-eye view, he saw: a striped rounded belly, four sets of tiny claws hooked into and desperately hanging onto the screen door and a little pink mouth wide open, howling. No doubt, it was howling for food but also because it was stuck in the screen door. Climbing up a screen door was, of course, easy but coming down was another matter. Human intervention made the earthbound trip less scary.

When the kittens were approximately three months old, Chicken suddenly monopolized the food on the communal plate, growling at her kittens to stay away until she had her fill. Puzzled, they had to wait their turn. She also swatted the kittens away when they attempted to nurse. Clearly, Mother was weaning her litter in no uncertain terms. Her unusual behaviour became clear to me when I saw her tummy becoming larger again. Another litter was on its way. She had taught these kittens all that she knew about survival; now they would have to venture forth and fend for themselves. Luckily, these beautiful kittens found new homes in the neighbourhood.

Chicken's next litter was born outside in the cold of winter. She nursed them only for a few days and then abandoned them, preferring to nest in a little wind shelter we had built for her on our front porch. For whatever reason her own instinct to survive became her first priority and sadly her litter died. Chicken was then apparently nine years old and I wondered about the numerous litters she must have borne during her lifetime. Was her advanced age the reason she abandoned her last litter? I spoke to our neighbour, offering to help pay for the cost of spaying Chicken but my offer was declined. Shortly after this conversation the family, taking Chicken along, moved.

Later that year, in July 1991, we also moved from our rented home and into our own. One year later out of nostalgia we decided to revisit the neighbourhood of our first home together. Coincidentally, during our walk, we saw an adult classic tabby roaming around our former home and recognized this handsome cat as one of Chicken's kittens that we had fed. Had a dim memory lured him back to his first home? Of course, he did not recognize us but we were delighted to see him looking healthy and hoped that his siblings had fared as well. We then reminisced about Chicken and sincerely wished that she had been spayed so that during her senior years all food consumed would be solely for her own benefit.

Kaze Kaiser Dickens

Darker than a Grand Knight

his eyes startling blue; two jewels in fur, dark of hue.

A luxurious Himalayan gown; taupe with points charcoal brown;

Kaze Kaiser Dickens.

Enigmatic; our Lord High Bushiness.

Games soared into gear as he conquered fear.

Ferocious during a Himalayan Charge, yet timid outside at large;

Kaze Kaiser Dickens.

After suffering from severe kidney malfunction, Dickens was euthanized on January 13, 1995, in the presence of those who loved him; George and his son Jeremy, my Mom and me. Dickens was only nine and a half years old. While we had the pleasure of his company for only five of those years, for us, they were a grand introduction into the mysteries of the feline world.

Born on June 6, 1985 and registered under the regal name of "Kaze Kaiser Dickens", he was affectionately known as "Dickens" but more often called "Dickie". Though registered, Dickie had not lived life as a show cat but as a pet. These few facts constitute our knowledge about the first four and a half years of his life but we do know everything about his life as of February 4, 1990, the date when he came into our lives. His life and ours changed dramatically. This story describes the auspicious set of circumstances that brought him into our lives and the years Dickens lived with us.

When George and I were living on Glynnhoven Road, I often wished we would get a cat. In fact George reminds me many times that I plaintively wailed, "I want a kitty!" He has never forgotten the tone of my voice. However, as much as I wished for a cat now that we rented a home with a backyard in which it could roam at will, the thought of our furniture and curtains etc. being shredded by an active kitten deterred us from further action. Although there are breeds that are hairless, bob-tailed and curly haired or eared, none have yet been bred without claws! The thought of being responsible for de-clawing a cat, sends shivers up my spine: I will not be responsible for such mutilation. We remained cat-less.

In our neighbourhood is a street named "Blossomfield Drive," a wonderful name that sent my imagination spinning. Sometimes to entertain George, I invented stories about Lord "Dickie" Blossomfield whose regiment was stationed in the Himalayas during Queen Victoria's reign. Lord "Dickie", a Major, was highly regarded by his peers for his daring exploits and admired by the rank and file whose rough life was made bearable by Lord Dickie's good nature and his generous purse. The Major's legacy shall continue to inspire generations while "Blossomfield Drive" exists, so I told George.

My cohorts at work knew that I really, really wanted a cat; preferably the long-haired type. One day my co-worker Peggy told me about a cat requiring a new home. She had all the particulars handy: a de-clawed, neutered five year old male, purebred Himalayan named Dickie. I could not believe my ears; my imaginary Lord "Dickie" of Himalayan fame had materialized; reincarnated into a furry Himalayan feline! Karma, coincidence or fate? My enthusiasm infected George who was a dog-lover and knew nothing about cats, but he is a darling indulging man and agreed we should find out all about this feline Himalayan Lord "Dickie"!

I was not familiar with the Himalayan breed but discovered that it is a cross between Persian and Siamese breeds. After several decades, this hybrid is now recognized and registered as a distinct breed. The Himalayan combines, in my opinion, the best features of both breeds: the Persian's stocky body shape, round eyes with its luxurious coat of long fur and the Siamese colour points with their stunning blue eyes. The Himalayan is apparently also well known for its gentle, docile, clownish playful nature.

We telephoned the owners who informed us that they wanted a new home for Dickens because their work commitment meant that Dickens was alone too often and for too long. Consequently, they were looking for a home where Dickens had more company. Other than our daily nine to five employment, we certainly considered ourselves homebodies. George's son, Jeremy, and daughter, Nicole, lived with us although the latter was studying art in Florence for one school year. We were all animal lovers. All in all, we felt we fulfilled the owners' requirements and made an appointment to meet our Himalayan "Lord Dickie"

As befitting his breed and lofty name, Dickens lived in a very fine home. The front foyer was larger than our living room and contained a full-sized grand piano. A very elegant mansion surrounded by lovely landscaped gardens, the size of which made it impossible to see either fence or shrubbery denoting property perimeters. While comfortably seated in the family room and with barely contained anticipation, we waited for "Lord Dickie" to present himself. In due time and without haste, our reincarnated hero made his appearance.

A most handsome distinguished looking Himalayan feline came into our presence. Intense Caribbean-blue eyes, nestled in rich dark brown seal-point coloured fur on his face, glanced casually at the strangers in his home. The body fur was a dark fall taupe colour and very dense; his coat was glorious. A thick bushy elegant tail wafted gently as he walked into the room. I noticed, dare I use such a mundane expression, the "cutest" long tufts between each front toe and underneath each hind paw. Beautifully proportioned, we were told he weighed fifteen pounds.

With his dark colouring and size, I worried that outside at night he might easily be mistaken for a racoon. When I voiced my concern, I was told that Dickens was strictly an indoor cat. He had never ever set even one of his genteel paws beyond the walls and doors of his home into the greater outside world. His confinement seemed very unnatural to me, especially since I think of cats as the essence of nocturnal hunters. I felt sad realizing he had no knowledge of the greater part of his natural world and quietly thought to myself that we might perhaps be instrumental in enlarging his world a little.

In addition to the "racoon" impression, Dickens' rear-view reminded me of a Cossack wearing dark brown boots with voluminous taupe pantaloons. He sported five inch whiskers, probably representative of the meticulously groomed Walrus mustachios sported by our imaginary "Lord Dickie Blossomfield". We thought Dickens was a most handsome Himalayan who lived up to his grand name; majestic, graceful and dignified. We were most impressed. While Lord Dickie appeared to be unimpressed with us, he was gracious enough to stay during our visit.

George and I would gladly adopt this handsome four and a half year old glorious fur ball and assured the owners that Kaze Kaiser Dickens' future well-being would be looked after to the best of our ability. Without further ado, Lord Dickie was placed inside his carrier and on the back seat of our tiny car along with his blanket, toys, food, litter box, brushes and other paraphernalia necessary for his well-being. The back seat was filled to overflowing! Catnapped from his home of four and a half years, Dickie howled piteously! And, with that traumatic experience began the trip to his new home.

Upon entering his new home, no matter how fearful, Lord Dickie's instinctive survival skills easily found the most inaccessible spot in our modest two-storey home: an alleyway, six inches wide and four feet long, behind Nicole's waterbed. Since she was away in Florence for one year, the alleyway became his hideaway: a sanctuary from this frightening unknown environment.

Dickens remained in his sanctuary and we left him in peace. Fresh water, food and his litter box were placed nearby. Each morning, before leaving for work, we left an extra little enticement at the entrance of his alleyway: one Kitty Love pill. It was gone when we got home in the late afternoon. Before going to bed at night, we left another Kitty Love pill. It too was gone in the morning. No other enticement was yet worth the great risk of leaving his sanctuary because nearby food, water and litter box remained untouched for three days!

Although we left him in peace to become accustomed to the new sounds of our household, I went into his room twice daily talking softly all the while. My cooing and cajoling did not bring him forth. Dickens remained safely hidden whenever we went into his room. Nothing was seen. Nothing was heard. Returning from a weekend away, Jeremy did not believe we had a new family member until he got down on all fours to look into the alleyway. All that he noticed was a phantom shadow from which piercing aqua blue spheres blinked periodically.

At last, on the fourth day Dickens ventured outside the safety of his alleyway to the nearby food bowl to nibble at his other favourite treat - tuna flavoured Tiny Morsels - and to use the litter box. Not that we saw him mind you, we only observed tell-tale signs. I breathed a sigh of relief realizing that Dickens needed plenty of time and continued patience to bring him out into the open.

Our work week was finally at an end. Oh, what bliss to sleep in on Saturday morning! That morning, the sixth day following his was catnapping, Dickens had become used to his early morning ration of Kitty Love pills. Had we forgotten; this would not do! A routine is a routine, not to be changed! Quietly, he ventured from his alleyway, out of his room, into the hallway at the bottom of the stairs leading to our bedroom and there discreetly let us know that he had been overlooked! At first, I thought I imagined his call and rolled over to sleep some more. His call became persistent and louder; no more sleep for me. Of course, as all animal lovers know, we humans, being easily trained, responded immediately! No more missed routines or sleeping in ever after.

The food was good, the water always fresh and the humans easily trained. Dangers anxiously anticipated for five days had not materialized. Perhaps life in this new home would not be so bad, after all. 'Were these Dicken' thoughts?' I wondered. Slowly our lives adapted and then games began. Dickens was chased around the house and up the stairs at which point all fifteen pounds of muscled furry ferocity turned to face the chaser. He was ready to execute Lord Dickie's infamous Himalayan Charge. Hair-raising human screams pierced the evening air. So much for the Himalayan docility! But then, this Himalayan was a reincarnation of our imaginary hero!

Boxes of all sizes also became a favourite entertainment. No matter what size, they had to be carefully investigated. More than once, Lord Dickie would try to fit his fifteen pound frame with two inch fur coat into a six inch square tissue box. His motto must have been, "If at first you do not succeed, try and try again!" All he managed to fit in were his legs. The rest of his body could not be persuaded inside and sat on top like a giant Portobello mushroom! One evening a large shallow cardboard box fell over him leaving only the front legs and tail exposed, giving the impression of a unique turtle whose evolution would have stumped even Charles Darwin. When the exposed legs or tail were tickled, this unique turtle moved with amazing speed and agility.

However, no matter what his pace or activity, Dickens' tail always wafted elegantly like a royal wave. We dubbed him with another pet name, "His Lord High Bushiness". Unlike some felines, Dickens was not fascinated by movement on the television screen nor his own image in a mirror. Imagery, movement or sound had to be "live" before it caught his attention. No chance of fooling our Lord High Bushiness!

Closed cupboards, on the other hand, were a totally different matter. What was inside?? A tufted paw would impatiently jiggle a door and a well-trained human would come running to open it and allow Lord Dickie to perform inspection duty. His were random surprise inspection tours; downstairs one day, upstairs another day. For this reason we simply had to keep the cupboards tidy otherwise we might be subjected to a derogatory sweep from his Lord High Bushiness' glorious tail.

Being an indoor cat, the "hunt" took a different form. In the absence of birds and mice, we humans became fair game. Ankles and calves were nipped, batted or pounced upon from behind doors or hidden corners. During these "hunts" it was suggested to Lord Dickie that he "be nice". We're certain he tried to curtail his instincts however each of us sports a little shredded flesh but our curtains and furniture remain unshredded! From observation and reading stories about other de-clawed cats, I have the feeling that they tend to bite more. Such behaviour makes perfect sense to me: in the absence of claws, teeth can "grab" quite nicely instead.

Paper bags were great fun too until one day the handles of one particular paper beast "attacked" Dickens by latching themselves over his head and around his neck! Chairs crashed to the floor as Dickens tried to evade the beast. Up and down the stairs he ran but the beast would not let go! At last, the beast lay shredded, bits and pieces everywhere amidst fallen chairs. Dickens left the battlefield triumphantly but quite some time was required before he regained his composure. Such a battle was never repeated; from then on paper bags, even those without handles, were carefully avoided.

Crumpled paper balls were the very best toys. With these, tennis or Ping-Pong was played. Of course, we well-trained humans did all the retrieving while Dickens batted the ball somewhere near your general direction. There must be dozens of used paper balls under unreachable spaces of couches and cupboards. Again with a paper ball, Dickens also enjoyed a game of basketball; easily catching your throw in mid-air by jumping several times his own length straight up in the air. In this manner, Lord Dickens kept his fine form battle-ready.

Being educated in the school of Natural Law, everything interested Dickens; from soap and running water in the bathroom to potatoes and vegetables in the kitchen. "Dickens, what is this?" I asked and without fail, he toddled over to inspect whatever object was in my hand. Once the inspection was over, Dickens returned to his favourite activity, sleeping on a spot warmed by the sun's rays or beside a heat register during wintertime.

To date, Dickens had acquired very specific gastronomic likes and dislikes. Tuna flavoured Tiny Morsels and Kitty Love pills were, to use an old expression, the cat's meow. A tiny tidbit of pork was acceptable as was a shred of Kentucky fried chicken. But, music to his ears was the sound of a tin being opened. Even when asleep, the opening of a tin and that tin possibly containing tuna brought Dickens hurriedly walking into our kitchen. Only tuna, thank you! Smoked oysters were an acceptable second choice but smoked salmon, shrimp or caviar were considered "hum-drum". Small dog biscuits, however, were considered irresistible; Dickens accepted a discreet half and trotted off somewhere private to fully enjoy his treat. A few crumbs were always left for us to vacuum.

When I wrote a letter, Dickens became my personal paperweight. Dickens was with me whenever I used the sewing machine and assisted by sitting on the fabric which allowed me to double-check that the stitches were straight and tiny! The taste of ribbons in the sewing box was delicious while buttons were boring. Old fashioned wooden spools were far more interesting than modern plastic spools. Much to my chagrin, vinyl covered measuring tapes were considered great chewing toys. Cork bottle stoppers were considered only mildly amusing toys.

Veterinarian Dr. Smythe fell in love with Dickens instantly and while he was always very good in her presence, he did prefer to be elsewhere, thank you very much! During the first consultation, on May 1990, we told her that Dickens had always eaten a prescription diet mixed with his favourite Tiny Morsels. Dr. Smythe sternly instructed us to discontinue feeding Tiny Morsels; "Yes, I know all cats love it but it's junk food; like potato chips." So, we obeyed her wise instructions.

One year later, Dickens developed a gastro-intestinal problem but under Dr. Smythe's excellent care, everything was soon under control and back to normal. Anxious to prevent a recurrence, we wanted to continue feeding whatever she had fed him. So I asked Dr. Smythe expecting to hear about a new prescription diet. Her answer was muffled, so I repeated my question. This time, head hung low, she confessed, "Tiny Morsels." "But you specifically forbade this food!!!" I replied exasperated. "I wanted to see if he was depressed" she answered, "but he was not." Apparently, she keeps a supply locked in the back of her desk just for that purpose!! After that enlightening tip, we too felt it prudent to check if Dickens was depressed every now and then; he never was.

We thought it was wonderful to see natural curiosity overcoming his anxiety in many ways. Just around his fifth birthday, Dickens ventured forth into the great outdoors for the first time. One beautiful sunny summer morning Jeremy was studying outside on the front steps leaving the door ajar. Overcoming his fear, Dickens followed his favourite human outside and there the two sat companionably together until a car drove by and Dickens scrambled back inside.

After his "outing", whenever we went outside, we left the back door leading into the garden open knowing that Dickens would want to be near us. From the doorway, he cried at us several times while we encouraged him to come to us. Grass blades must have tickled his tufted paws because it took several hesitant attempts before one tufted paw remained firmly planted on the grass, cautiously followed by three other tufted paws. Hardened earth was also carefully tested before being judged safe enough to tread upon. Since his delicate five year old paws had only ever felt smooth parquet floors, soft broadloom and fine Persian carpets, his caution was natural.

The outdoors was a truly new world. Eventually his feet toughened and he patrolled outside his new home. A favourite spot, from which to survey his domain, was the milk-box, long since abandoned for its original purpose. During warm summer days, we left both doors of the milk-box open for Dickens' use.

He sat there for hours watching everything; his frame filling a good three-quarters of the milk-box whose inside dimensions measured about a cubic foot.

At the same time, he also developed an awareness of other felines but since none of them belonged to his own lofty breed, a slight glance from a distance was considered a sufficient greeting. Since Dickens' first five years were solitary, I was not surprised that he did not approach other felines but I found it interesting that they did not approach him either. I wondered if Dickie's lack of interest would ever change and sure enough, it did.

One evening we were sitting outside with Dickens and observed our neighbour's cat, named Chicken, enticing the attentions of a male suitor. Suddenly to our great surprise, Dickens executed his infamous Himalayan charge upon Chicken's unsuspecting suitor. The chase took both males across the street where a standoff took place. Luckily the suitor, who was much smaller than Dickens, wisely retreated before anything serious developed. We found Dickens' reaction totally unexpected and wondered whether he was protecting Chicken or just his own territory.

Nevertheless, Chicken became pregnant and since she was left to fend mostly for herself, was constantly hungry. If she was able to access Dickens' food bowl in our kitchen, she would, whereupon a short scuffle erupted. In her pregnant state, Chicken would not risk becoming injured and quickly left the food bowl to its owner. Based on Dickens' behaviour in this instance, I suspect he was not feeling protective towards Chicken when he chased away her suitor but simply protecting his own territory.

Other than chasing away Chicken's suitor, Dickens did not wander far when outside and showed no interest in what lay beyond the perimeters of our property, thank goodness! Nor was he inclined to stay outside by himself, preferring to be in our company which was just as well, given his lack of claws.

Better than chasing paper balls indoors, was chasing insects or butterflies outdoors. June bugs, flies and spiders had a certain crunchy appeal: just the thing to whet his appetite but when Blue Jays dive-bombed Dickens to protect their young, birds were considered dangerous and avoided just like those beastly paper bags. And then, joy of joys, Dickens found fresh catnip in the garden: oh those lazy summer days, satiated with catnip, then sleeping in the warmth of the afternoon sun. What a change from the cautious indoor cat; surely, his life had become fuller and more interesting?

One hot summer evening during dinner, Dickens was chasing a huge blue-bottle fly which naturally was attracted to the scent of food. As the fly flew over the dinner table, Dickens jumped onto a chair after the fly; an instant later a huge taupe fur ball flew over the dining table in hot pursuit of the fly without touching a dish! With open mouths we watched this scene! If a camera had captured that scene, I'm certain it would have won first prize. Dickens caught and relished his appetizer. Nicole, George's daughter, became nauseated, and left the table. What a memorable family dinner!

Other than that incident Dickens never jumped onto a chair, couch, bed or lap. We assumed that in his previous home, furniture was out of bounds for him and he had learnt well. We did not feel that way; we felt, our home was his and that meant Dickens was free to pick his own perfect spot. It took about a year for Dickens to accept this new freedom but he did learn.

Except for the occasional meaow, we never heard Dickens purr and thought perhaps his breed lacked that capability but about two years after Dickens came into our lives, we finally heard a soft discreet purr that eventually became a peeping rumble. To our ears, Dickens unique purr was a very rewarding sound. During the last three years he purred frequently and rested on chairs or our bed. If we were sitting on a couch, Dickens rested beside us after having "kneaded and softened" the area thoroughly but to our dismay, he never sat on our laps. Previously, we had the impression that all cats were lap-cats but Dickens taught us differently.

George and Dickens developed a ritual prior to our bedtime. Dickens was asked, "Are you ready to go to bed?" whereupon he preceded George upstairs into our bedroom, jump onto a corner of the bed and settle comfortably. George then stroked him gently generating the long awaited purr. However, like all cats, Dickens was a nocturnal creature, and after a few minutes of pleasing his human, Dickens jumped off our bed, raced down the stairs and into the living room expecting to be chased by George who, naturally accommodated. George was easily trained.

Dickens became, in George's words, a "mush-bucket". Shamelessly flopping at your feet and spread-eagled on his back was his definitive signal for more attention or that it was play-time...everyone's at home, let the games begin! In preparation for the fun to come was his ritual "sharpening" his long-gone-claws; a ritual that never ceased.

Even though we encouraged Dickens to roost wherever he wished, there was a disadvantage. His thick, long dense taupe coloured fur coated every piece of furniture upon which he rested. The colour change was very subtle until you realized that all the furniture and carpeting appeared to be the same colour! A thorough vacuum was in order again. Now, I am not the world's best housekeeper; far from it, therefore I gratefully accepted some wise words from Dr. Smythe who advised us: "If you want an immaculate home, do not own a pet." Ah well, we feel that a less than spotless home was a small sacrifice for Kaze Kaiser Dickens.

Another habit Dickens had was to hide in fear after expelling a hairball. I wondered why he was fearful, when vomiting a hairball was a normal occurrence for long-haired cats. Each time, it took some time to coax him out into the open and assure him all was well. Again with patience, his behaviour changed. During the last year or so, while I cleaned up the mess, generally at 4:30AM during the week, Dickens sat companionably nearby blinking encouragingly.

One morning in October 1992, Dickens refused to jump down from his favourite chair to eat breakfast. Instead, he remained curled up. We saw nothing wrong and placed him on the floor; poor Dickens limped back to the chair, jumped up and curled up again. An X-ray at the Veterinarian revealed a fracture in the left hind leg. Instead of a cast, tight sutures kept the leg straight and his fur between hock and upper thigh was shaved off. During the healing process of about six weeks, we were instructed not to let him jump but this was impossible. Even with a stiff leg he managed to get wherever he wished. Our Dickens looked most unsightly and undignified when one hind leg resembled a plucked drumstick !

Of course, his leg healed beautifully but the cause of his fracture is a mystery. I believe that he slid along a bare wooden floor chasing a toy and crashed into a bi-fold door, causing his hind leg to become wedged between the door and floor. As he wrenched his leg out from this narrow space at an odd angle, a fracture occurred. Oh, what pain he must have suffered and, of course, in silence.

George and I decided to drive north of Toronto to the Severn River area for a weekend during the fall of 1994. The colours were at their best and the weather was wonderful. We were grateful, that my Mom offered to take care of Dickens for us. Although we had visited Mom at her home with Dickens before, we had no idea how he would react to a weekend visit at her home. Favourite toys, foods and blankets etc. were brought over as well and George and I bade our goodbyes.

Apparently Dickens felt catnapped again because he hid. Mom could not find him anywhere in her two-storey home but she felt he was in her bedroom. Mom then had a brilliant idea; after a few hours of leaving him in peace, she opened a tin of tuna and walked into her bedroom, called to him and simply waited until the smell of tuna pervaded her bedroom. That scent was more than Dickens could bear...slowly he emerged from his hiding place and accepted her offering of his favourite food. When we returned from our weekend away, Dickens was comfortably asleep on Dad's chair opposite Mom who was reading. It had been a good weekend for everyone.

Since Dickens had been an only pet, we sometimes mused about his reaction to a feline companion and by chance, a companion for him entered our lives when we rescued a starving blind stray in October 1994. We named her "Princess" and with care she thrived. When she was brought inside, the two cats were slowly introduced to each other. Of course initially, there was the usual hissing and spitting but eventually, they got used to each other. Dickens must have thought her very odd walking into walls and chairs etc. but she certainly wasn't afraid to retaliate and swat him when he had the misfortune to sit in her path! He accepted her odd behaviour with good grace and gave up favourite sleeping spots and his food bowl, but even Dickens retaliated when Princess searched through his toy box! Completely opposite in breed, character and size, we dubbed them Mr. Puffit and Ms. Muffit.

During a celebration just prior to Christmas in 1994, our cats were "dressed" with beautiful red bows to greet our guests. Princess always allowed us to tie a bow without any problem and on this occasion so did Dickens, who normally did not like anything around his neck. The fact that he accommodated us this time seemed an indication that he was mellowing in his old age. But that was not the case as we discovered.

Two days before Christmas, Dickens lost interest in food and slept even longer than his normal 20 hours per day. Usually his disinterest in food indicated a hairball problem but after we medicated him with a remedy, his lethargy remained. He slept and did not eat. We wondered whether he could be depressed about the permanent presence of Princess. However considering the fact that they had been sitting together touching noses, we realized her presence couldn't be the source of his problem either. After two days of not eating and sleeping almost non-stop, we became worried and took action.

Off to Dr. Smythe again. Blood tests indicated severe kidney malfunction. The blood urea nitrogen level was 50 compared to the norm of 4-10, and the creatinine level was at 700 compared to the norm of 150! Initially with medication and intravenous feeding, Dickens rallied and we brought him home for Christmas but his improved condition was short-lived. Over a period of three weeks, he had eaten what he normally would in two days and his weight loss was noticeable. His fur was dull and his eyes lacklustre. What cruel irony, as quickly as Princess was gaining health, Dickens was losing his. It was obvious that his kidneys were no longer functioning. Dickens had already suffered for three weeks, and we knew from his appearance and behaviour that he must have felt very, very sick. Without prolonging his misery, there was only one option. With heavy hearts and in the presence of those who loved him, Dickens was put to sleep.

Dickens was with us almost five years to the day and in retrospect these years seemed short and went by far too fast. To us he was truly a thoroughbred; dignified, regal, aloof and handsome. Likewise he was a clown; playful, mischievous, inquisitive and affectionate. We miss him much more than anticipated but eventually will remember with pleasure our most glorious pet. As Dickens added much enjoyment to our lives, we believe we succeeded in enlarging his world and adding interest, companionship and entertainment to his life.

Princess

The Cat Who Came in from the Cold

Princess, not regal nor proud,
so determined to live;
ultimate testament to feline endurance.

> Overcoming barriers of sight and time,
> so determined to live,
> survived hunger and clime.

> Her ninth life transcended,
> now basking forever,
> in the warmth of her heavenly Sun.

This story is about an extraordinary cat that came into our lives one cold October evening; Saturday, October 28, 1994, to be precise. Princess shared the last two years of her life with us during which time we learned much more about felines and she, in turn, gave us her trust and affection.

As we made our customary amble around our garden after work on Friday, October 27, 1994, George and I felt winter's chill in the air. Dickens, His Lord High Bushiness, followed close behind. With collars up around our necks, bemoaning the passing of fall and not particularly looking forward to the long winter ahead, we noticed an unfamiliar cat in the yard next door.

It was white with grey patches, small and of the short-haired variety. Unlike most cats, this one seemed to be wandering aimlessly without a specific purpose. It walked in a peculiar manner dragging its hind quarters very low to the ground. Being "cat people", we naturally called the cat and it came towards us. Unfortunately, Dickens had also seen the cat and began his infamous Himalayan charge stopping about a foot away from the cat that crouched and froze, huddled against our neighbour's house. We thought Dickens' behaviour odd; why did he stop and what did he realize that we did not?

The cat must have been aware of Dickens and appeared to have become very frightened. Not wishing to add to its obvious distress, we scooped up Dickens and brought him inside our home. Curious, we went outside again only to see the cat slowly crawling against the wall towards the front of our neighbour's house. Again, we called the cat but this time we were ignored. We continued to watch for a while and noticed it seemed unsure about its path. Eventually George and I went inside our own warm home, but our thoughts remained focussed on this sad little creature and if it was a stray, then we hoped it had a warm shelter somewhere that very, very cold night.

The following day, Saturday, October 28th, was a beautiful, bright sunny morning although the temperature was close to freezing. Immediately after coffee, we went outside to see if this pathetic creature was still around, and, yes, there it was in the yard behind ours. Curled up, cat fashion it was lying in the sun, warming itself. At one point, it seemed to reach out with its paw and catch something to chew on, an insect? We watched it for a while and called but were given no response.

Hours later, after we had run our usual Saturday errands, we saw that this cat was in the same place. We observed it once more and agreed that at least to our knowledge, this cat just did not move or behave in normal cat-like manner. We couldn't define exactly why its movements were odd until we saw it walking straight into the fence, not once, but several times: it was blind! No wonder its movements were hesitant and cautious.

Blindness was likely the reason it walked against the house wall to give itself a sense of direction. Blindness was also likely the reason it walked in a crouched position to give itself leverage should the front legs go into a hole. It couldn't hunt; therefore it ate insects or whatever crawled in the path of its claws.

Oh, the poor creature! Was it lost or abandoned? How long had it been outside on its own? Even if a blind cat was able to defend itself against other cats or worse, how much longer could it do so without regular food? For how much longer could it retain life against winter's colder nights and days without a proper shelter?

Well, now that we knew this cat was blind, we agreed not to leave it outside on its own any longer. Our neighbour, in whose yard this cat had entrapped itself, came outside and he told us he had noticed this cat wandering around for several days already. No-one in his area recognized this cat and he had intended to bring the cat to our local shelter. Because the cat wore an old leopard print collar, we realized it must have been someone's pet. Unfortunately, the collar did not have any identifying tags, therefore ownership was a mystery.

We asked our neighbour to hand the cat over to us so that we could feed the poor thing; it probably hadn't had much to eat or drink, perhaps for a very long time. Once in George's arms, we could see every vertebrae of the spine protruding. Skin and bones! The cat was the size of a six months old kitten; perhaps it was, who knew? Intuition told us our mystery cat was female. We could not possibly risk bringing her into our house with Dickens as she would certainly be flea-ridden and possibly also diseased. We decided to keep her in our garage while we a considered a practical long-term solution.

I got busy feeding her; she wolfed down the soft food placed before her and drank a little water as well. In the meantime, George got busy making a warm bed for her in our garage, out of a cardboard box which he lined with insulation and old woolly sweaters. This box was placed, not directly on the cold cement garage floor, but on a full piece of insulation: it would be warm and dry. Food, water and a litter box were placed nearby.

George carried her into the garage, showed her the litter box, food, water and her new bed. She promptly crawled into her new bed, curled up and went to sleep. Exhausted! Could it have been the first safe, sound sleep she fell into, in who knows how long a period of time; days, weeks perhaps months? Who knew? We thought it was interesting that she didn't fight being held, indicating to us that she was certainly familiar with humans. What on earth had happened to her?

After dinnertime we went into the garage, to check on our little guest and discovered that she had eaten all the food and was asleep again. Rather than using the litter box, she had chosen as her toilet wood shavings located on the other side of the garage. The poor thing had terrible diarrhoea. Her sense of aesthetics was more refined than ours, for who would want their toilet beside their food? Point taken: we moved her litter box as she had indicated. More food and fresh water were left beside her bed.

George and I felt that under normal circumstances a blind cat would remain within familiar territory. Even if it had wandered away a little, wouldn't such a cat have a very good sense of direction and find its way back home? Surely those living beside the home of a blind cat would be aware of it? No one in our area seemed to know and we concluded that the cat belonged in another neighbourhood. Had she wandered too far away or had something caused her to become disoriented? Saturday evening, we drove around the neighbourhood looking for "Lost Cat" signs. We found nothing. Was she then deliberately abandoned? I couldn't fathom such cruelty but as a friend commented to me, "Lotte, people abandon their children; why not their pet?"

Just before going to bed, we checked on our feline guest again. This time, at the sounds of our voices, she awakened, crawled out of her warm bed towards us and cried. Well now, we have heard many modulations of cats' meaows, but never had we heard a meaow like hers. The closest description, if you will imagine, is a meaow whose owner has a severe case of laryngitis. Such a hoarse whispery squawk from such a small feline! George picked her up and she just seemed to melt in the comfort of his warm arms. She squawked in response to everything uttered to her... we kept thinking this kitty must have been loved very much by someone... she was so responsive. What a mystery!

We realized that speculation about the circumstances that brought her into our lives could last forever without ever being resolved but, right now, our only focus should be towards helping her to regain health. Her state was pitiable!

She walked with a drunken sideways lurch dragging her hind quarters while her tail hung like a wet lifeless strand of spaghetti. When positioned over the food or water bowl, her front legs jerked in a spastic manner. We wondered whether this condition was due to a nerve problem or related to paralysis? Denuded of fur by incessant pawing, her nose ran like a faucet; likewise her eyes watered constantly. Did these symptoms represent a common cold or something much more serious? One eye was blue and the other green; both appeared normal to us but obviously she was blind. Was her blindness related to something very serious? Were all these conditions due to starvation or was she mortally ill? Had she been abandoned to avoid huge vet bills?

The following day on Sunday we took her to an emergency clinic for a professional evaluation. Considering the deprivation she had endured, we hoped the prognosis would be positive requiring only patience, good care, food and shelter. If so, then we were prepared to provide exactly that. Additionally, we hoped that, once nursed back to health, this pretty feline would become a companion to our solitary Dickens. However, if the conclusion was that this cat was mortally ill and ought to be put to sleep, then we were prepared to accept that responsibility.

The first visit to the veterinarian's office confirmed that "our" kitty was a female, weighed only six pounds, was dehydrated, spayed and estimated to be between four and six years old. We were delighted that our intuition regarding gender was correct but surprized to hear that our little female was a mature lady.

A stool examination proved she didn't have worms but the poor creature was anaemic due to a severe flea infestation and until she had gained some weight, it was considered prudent to delay drawing a blood sample to determine the presence of feline diseases. We accepted that an immediate flea bath was necessary and we agreed to feed her "developmental" food along with a vitamin supplement.

The runny nose, eyes and laboured breathing were symptoms of a chest cold which the veterinarian believed would clear itself within ten days; especially since she would now be eating a very nourishing diet, otherwise antibiotics would be prescribed. Her diarrhoea was likely due to a change in food; specifically from none to plenty. After a long sabbatical from regular feedings, her digestive system was now working overtime and, again, it was felt that her loose bowels would correct themselves over time.

During this examination, it was noticed that her pupils responded to light but not movement and George asked whether her blindness could be a temporary condition due to starvation. The vet believed their resident ophthalmologist could provide us with an answer and we were scheduled to speak with him during our next visit.

From her overall condition, the veterinarian concluded she had managed on her own for at least six months. That she survived in the face of the most trying obstacles, is surely a testament to a cat's perseverance, ingenuity and remarkable survival instincts? We all hoped that with good food etc., most of her conditions, including the spastic movements in her legs would decrease or, hopefully, disappear. Of course, only the results of a blood sample, yet to be drawn, would determine whether or not she was free of disease but we were relieved that no suggestion was made to put her to sleep.

So far she had been handled by several strangers, including ourselves, yet she did not mind at all. We concluded that she had not suffered abuse and must have been well-loved.

We went home feeling encouraged by the results of the visit but left our new pet behind to drown the host of fleas to which she had provided an uninvited home! We could pick her up the following evening on Monday and were warned to thoroughly wash or preferably discard anything on which she had slept.

On the way home we started discussing a name for her. We felt that this special feline deserved a name to match her courage and tenacity. In addition, her name would have to be suitably lofty to match that of our registered purebred Himalayan named "Dickens; His Lord High Bushiness". We chose the name, "Princess, the cat who came in from the cold". Her name on the vet's files could be changed from "No Name" to "Princess".

While Princess was being deflead , George was thinking about constructing an improved shelter for her in our garage, taking into account that it might be weeks before she could come into our home and that the nights were becoming colder. It should be insulated, heated, vented and temperature controlled. A "Princess Palace" was designed and constructed by an architectural technologist, my softy husband, George.

The design was ingenious: an inverted box, lined with insulation, set on four bricks, one under each corner. The ground floor had a cutaway entrance from where Princess climbed a three brick stairway to her sleeping loft that was lined with a mohair scarf. Heat was provided by a 40 Watt bulb, inside a safety construction lamp that hung in a corner opposite her "bed" and a thermometer hung on the other corner. The roof was a thick plastic sheet attached with clips that could be undone to allow venting if necessary and as required by code! This "sky-light" of a roof allowed us to view our sleeping Princess and even though it was freezing in the garage, the temperature inside her palace was a toasty 70 degrees Fahrenheit. Yes indeed, the "Princess Palace" was a very comfortable loft wherein she could sleep and heal. What an amazing structure…maybe this ought to be patented.

But, we had one concern. If the light bulb should fail during freezing weather, heat loss would be immediate and that could prove to be a setback to Princess' health. During the day we would know quickly since we visited several times but what about at night? How could we be alerted? Well, as always, George thought of a practical solution. A mirror was placed strategically on our car roof so that we could see the lamp's reflection through the garage window from our bedroom window. Since we each wake up periodically during the night, we each checked regularly that the bulb was lit. A bulb did burn out once; George put on his coat, went outside to the garage, replaced the bulb and then came back to bed.

Hold on and back up, I am getting ahead of myself because Princess was still undergoing her fleabath. We could hardly wait to pick her up on Monday evening, October 31, 1994. What a difference a little grooming had made, she looked so clean. Apparently the flea infestation had been so severe that a second flea bath might be necessary and so, a second appointment was made for the following week during which her general condition would be monitored and she could be examined by the ophthalmologist.

It might have been our imaginations, but we felt Princess recognized our voices and was glad we hadn't abandoned her. While we talked, she squawked hoarsely at us and purred. Home we drove with a clean cat, prescription developmental food and vitamin supplements. Now Princess would have to do her bit.

The night we brought Princess home was October 31, 1994; it was also Halloween. It was a miserable windy dark evening with freezing rain. I remain convinced that if Princess

44

not been rescued, she would have died that night. As it was, she literally had both hind legs in the grave. I do not believe her weakened body could have survived Halloween's nasty weather. But, as is known, a cat has nine lives and certainly Princess was given a new lease on life: sheltered, fed and protected. A few days had already made such a difference!

The Princess Palace, cozy and warm, awaited its new owner. Incredibly, she needed guidance up and into her warm nest only once! After that she went up and down by herself without ever missing a step. An amazing feat for a blind kitty we thought: indeed a Princess.

Three times per day the food bowl was filled and consumed. I couldn't believe the amount she was eating but then she was making up for lost time. No doubt, an awful lot of repair work was being done inside her little body. Princess was doing her bit with gusto. As her body adjusted to regular feedings, changes indicating better health appeared. She became calmer, walked a little straighter and we thought we detected a tiny movement in her inexpressive tail. The diarrhoea finally stopped after six days. Her voice became a little less hoarse but her vocal chords retained their chronic laryngitis quality.

The second vet visit, one week later, indicated no need for a second flea bath, but because the flea infestation had been severe, Princess was dewormed, just to be on the safe side. She certainly didn't need that problem: all the food she consumed must be for her benefit alone. Although the vet remarked she looked and seemed to be feeling better, any weight gain was yet immeasurable. A blood sample was taken during this visit but because her blood was still "thin", it did not clot quickly. The results of the blood tests confirmed she was free of disease: what a relief! We would bring her inside our home once the lingering "cold" symptoms disappeared.

During this vet visit, Princess was examined by the resident ophthalmologist. Upon placing her on the examination table, he asked us if she had claws. "Yes, she does" we answered. "Hold her tight" he commanded. We thought his response was rather amusing and wondered if he was afraid of being clawed or just cautious about his hands. We felt it was the former and wondered why he would be involved with felines. However, he seemed to know what he was doing as he examined her eyes. He told us that her left retina was missing most likely due to an inherited condition. In all probability she had been blind since birth. Although his diagnosis provided us with an answer, it wasn't what we had hoped to hear. We accepted that if she had been sightless since birth, then that condition was normal for her; blindness didn't appear to be causing her any stress.

Her respiratory infection continued; her breathing was still laboured while her nose and eyes continued to water. It was the first time I had ever observed a cat with a cold, and was surprised that the symptoms were similar to a human cold. Isolation was recommended for at least two more weeks and thanks to George's ingenious design, continued lodging in the Princess Palace would be more than acceptable, thank you very much! At last, on November 18, 1994, three weeks after she had found us, her cold symptoms were slowly disappearing and she was no longer contagious.

It was time to bring her inside our home and introduce her to Dickens who had been very intrigued by the fact that we entered the garage frequently while his entry was barred. Of course, as all cat lovers know, there is nothing more interesting to a cat than a forbidden place! Dickens was intrigued.

Princess was brought into our guest room which now contained a new wicker basket with soft towels, her food and water bowls and, as far away as possible from the food dishes, her litter box. All of this activity was of great interest to Dickens. Within five minutes, the two cats became aware of each other whereupon a healthy exchange of sniffing, hissing and spitting occurred; all of this through a narrow opening beneath the closed bedroom door. Well now, each knew where the other was located; this would become interesting!

Antibiotics were prescribed to clear up the lingering respiratory infection on her third visit to the veterinarian's office. Her weight gain was steady with another added pound; she was now seven pounds. At this stage, she was no longer wolfing down her food, as though there were no tomorrow, but eating in a normal manner. One could actually see an improvement in the texture of fur, even a very thin layer of fat could be felt. Regardless of improvement, we were advised to have a little more patience before injecting her with all the normal feline shots.

Her tail and other jerky movements remained a concern. When held horizontally, it jerked spasmodically so violently that it hit her hind quarters causing her to cry out. Whether her cry was due to pain or surprise, no one knew; perhaps a bit of both. Her hind quarters must have been sensitive because she became apprehensive whenever she was touched in that area. Whenever she positioned herself over the water/food bowls, her front legs jerked involuntarily and we wondered whether these involuntary actions between legs and tail were related. Was this nerve or muscle damage? What was its cause?

At last, on November 26th, her fourth visit to the vet, she was considered strong enough to tolerate all the required feline immunization shots. However, the serums must have hit her system like a thunderbolt because she slept like a log for two days. We woke her several times to make sure she ate.

Whenever George and I were at home, we allowed Princess to wander through the house at will. There were no serious confrontations with Dickens but he must have found it very puzzling when she walked into him and then, swatted him for having the effrontery to be in her pathway! Dickens, however wronged he was, remained the perfect gentleman and never hit his lady. He must have decided it was prudent to stay out of her way and took to occupying the rear portion of the house while she took charge of the front portion. Had this arrangement between the two cats been one of telepathic communication? When we were unable to keep an eye on them, Princess was put back into her own room.

One time, her room was needed for a visiting family member. Princess was moved into our den, which has no door, so for her nightly confinement, the doorway was blocked with a piece of insulation approximately three feet high. Though her hind quarters were too weak for jumping, she had extraordinary strength in her front legs. In no time, she had shredded the insulation barrier and easily climbed over its remains. She had reached freedom! Princess had clearly informed us in no uncertain terms, that she no longer wished to be confined to any room. We thanked her for sharing this information with us!

Now, free to investigate the main floor, Princess discovered our soft warm waterbed. Of all the space available on this queen size surface, she decided that Dickens' favourite spot would be hers. Gentleman that he was, Dickens relinquished his spot just as he had his food and water bowls. Did he wonder though whether her imperious manner indicated that she was a queen rather than a mere princess? Regardless, he would not give up his toy box, no sir; enough is enough! A short boxing match erupted and Princess retreated to play with her own toy, a bell wrapped in paper. Sometimes Dickens postured playfully, on his back, in front of her but blind Princess continued on her way stumbling over him. Her behaviour was baffling to Dickens.

By early December 1994, she had gained another pound and was now a respectable eight pounds. A layer of fat was visible and her hind quarters seemed a little less sensitive: things continued to improve.

Once Princess was completely familiar with the main floor, we thought to introduce her to the stairs leading to the basement where Dickens' litter box was stationed and to where hers would be moved. The day that her litter box was brought downstairs, I first carried her and then coaxed her four times into following me to its new location. Naturally, negotiating the curved stairway was tricky. During the first three attempts, she stumbled and while her dignity was ruffled, she was unhurt. During the fourth attempt, Princess successfully negotiated the stairs and, to my amazement, reached her litter box and promptly used it!

She loved being outdoors. During sunny warm days, Princess easily found the perfect sheltered spot and here we placed a two inch piece of Styrofoam board along with a bowl of water. Princess then stepped onto her little platform, curled up or stretched out for a luxurious nap in the sun. "Thank you and please wake me for dinner. Oh, perhaps a treat just now would be just lovely!" Surely life with us was quite satisfactory.

For walks outside, we purchased a pink harness and leash which she accepted without any trouble. Likely, it gave her a bearing that was otherwise lacking. Weather permitting, Princess was led around our garden and street every day. Our neighbours were puzzled by this eccentric sight until informed about her blindness.

During walks down the driveway and onto the street, George noticed that Princess always turned eastward. A tantalizing clue: was she instinctively heading towards her previous home? Of course, we never would find out. Although we still watched for "Lost Cat" notices, none were ever seen, nor did our local vet hear anything. At this point, I must confess that we might have ignored such notices because Princess had claimed our hearts.

One other tantalizing clue was observed during one of our daily strolls. Princess was generally fearless about outside noises from other people, dogs, cars or delivery trucks, taking them all in stride. The only exception was the sound made by the sturdy work boots; these of course produced more noise than shoes. Princess' reaction was extraordinary; she actually strained at the leash wanting to run in the opposite direction. What ingrained memory caused her reaction, had she been severely kicked? Was this an explanation for the sensitivity in her hind quarters? I picked her up immediately to provide comfort and waited until the "danger" had passed before we continued our stroll.

The ophthalmologist, who had already examined her eyes in January 1995, asked our permission to photograph her unusual eyes because he wished to consult a colleague. We agreed. Their consensus was that Princess was likely born sighted but lost it early in life due to degenerative retinal disease.

During this visit, an X-ray taken of her hind quarters finally provided an answer to her sensitivity in that region. It revealed that the left femur was dislocated outside the hip socket as well as a healed fracture of the left leg near the pelvis. Arthritic deformation in that area was clearly visible. Lastly, it revealed a smashed spine at the point of entry through the pelvis: this injury would have affected the nerve endings thus explaining the spastic movements of her tail and legs. The vet suggested that "blunt trauma" possibly from a vehicle was the likely cause of her injuries, if true, we wondered why she seemed totally unafraid of cars and trucks.

Surgically, her left leg could be placed back into its socket providing her with more mobility and comfort. However, that meant keeping her immobile inside a cage for six weeks while she healed. We decided against surgery because she struggled desperately whenever she was placed inside the cat carrier; we felt that six weeks of confinement would be unbearable for her. Instead, we would keep her as comfortable as possible for as long as possible. We rarely saw her jump likely because it was too painful. Instead, climbing was her preferred mode and as can be imagined, her front legs, shoulders and chest were very powerful.

When Princess finally reached 8.5 pounds, she had probably reached her ideal weight because a layer of fat was evident and, finally, her "developmental" diet was replaced with a "maintenance" diet. Her fur sported a healthy sheen; pure white underneath with large grey spots on the sides and back. Life settled into a routine with naps in the sun and escorted walks outside. Inside, nutritious food was always available and a choice of human laps onto which Princess scrambled on to drool and purr with contentment.

During Christmas 1994, as Princess was gaining her health, very sadly, Dickens was losing his due to kidney malfunction. He was put to sleep in early January 1995. Now alone, we believed, Princess felt Dickens' loss as well. Even though the two had not become friends, there had been "friendly" (??) boxing matches over choice spots on the sofa or a favourite chair. Alone, Princess meaowed and wandered around more than usual; was she calling Dickens? Perhaps, in her mind, even nuisance company was preferable to none but emotionally, George and I were not yet ready to consider a new companion for Princess; perhaps later.

Ever since her rescue, a small white sliver was seen protruding from the center of her lower jaw. Upon examination it proved to be a small benign tumour that was surgically removed in March 1995. While under anaesthetics her teeth were examined and a broken lower right molar was removed. Tough old lady came home a bit wobbly and weak from the after effects of the anaesthetic but other than that, just fine, thank you very much!

Two months later in May 1995, George and I relented as Solomon, a Himalayan kitten, came into our lives. We thought that feline company would be good stimulation for Princess. Well, in retrospect, the rambunctious antics of a young kitten were too much for her. While Solomon immediately took to his Princess, she rebuffed his attention and, alas, his lot in life was one of unrequited love. She may not have wanted Solomon around but we did. He was here to stay!

And so, spring progressed into summer. Princess loved being outdoors in the sun and learned to open the screen door leading to our patio and garden, clawing into the screen and pulling it to one side; in and out as she pleased. Taking full advantage of this opportunity, Solomon followed his clever Princess, happily gambolling around her.

Because our backyard wasn't fenced, we didn't think that allowing our cats to wander freely at will was a good idea. Princess accepted being tethered for naps in the sun but young Solomon struggled frantically against a similar restraint. What could we do? Finally our brilliant idea was to cordon off our patio with a white plastic mesh fence allowing both cats ten square feet of space in which to wander. Surely that was enough room but it wasn't! Princess had other ideas, resented being restrained and clawed through the mesh fence, down the patio steps and into the garden for another "free range" stroll. Most impressed with Princess' Houdini-like skills, Solomon leisurely padded after her to inspect the garden and beyond before we brought them both back. We locked the screen door. Afterwards, when outside, both cats were tethered and Solomon eventually accepted.

During one of Princess' "free range" strolls, we observed a remarkable sight. Hearing birds chirping, her hunting instinct took over and crouched as low as possible, she ran towards the chirping birds. Of course, her "hunt" was unsuccessful but wasn't it amazing that instinct superseded blindness? We wondered whether she had ever hunted successfully.

With her health stabilized, we ceased using the emergency clinic that was a half hour away by car. Instead, we took Princess to our local vet who is only two blocks away from home. Our local veterinarian is a man of few words and other than the obligatory greeting, his concentration is totally upon examining the pet. But oh, is he eloquent with our furry friends! Granted, they don't like him more than any other doctor but it is wonderful to see his calm and gentle manner with our pets. His skill with animals and lack of same with their owners is well known in our neighbourhood! I admire him; recommending only what is best for the animal even if inconvenient for the owner.

Unknown to us, at the time of adoption, was the fact that Solomon had ringworm. Princess became afflicted and so did we. Our entire home required "cleansing". The prescribed treatment that eventually worked for both cats was a monthly bath with a special shampoo. We were very apprehensive about bathing Princess so George and I were prepared for a tough battle with an unwilling blind cat. Surprise, surprise, Princess loved the warm water! Perhaps it soothed her arthritic bones and drying had to be done gently with towels and a hair dryer. However, this shampoo tinted Princess' white fur yellow. I wonder what our neighbours thought of a yellow/grey cat on a leash. Never mind, I'm certain Princess was glad to be rid of the itching, regardless of the temporary colour of her fur.

Princess was a true lap-cat; she loved to sit on your lap. Comfortably perched she drooled and "talked" and by that I mean, she made a lip-smack sound followed by an "aaaghh" sound. I responded similarly (yes, I did) and our conversation was repeated some half dozen times. George once asked what we were talking about, and I told him our conversation was private girl talk!

If one of us was having an afternoon nap, she climbed onto the bed and your body walking all over before nestling either in the crook of your arm or on top of your chest, again drooling. We kept a little towel handy just to catch the drool drops. With Princess and Solomon on our bed, George and I were lucky to find some space for ourselves! We once tried to keep the cats outside by closing our door. Well, their howling was worse than us trying to find space, so the bedroom door remained open.

As time went on, we noticed blood in her stool or very loose stools without any change in her diet. In November 1995, blood was drawn to check her kidney function and indeed the tests confirmed elevated levels of blood urea nitrogen and creatinine: her kidneys were no longer functioning well. To try and stabilize the stress on her kidneys, a modified diet of chicken with rice was suggested followed by prescription "kidney diet".

Over the next year, the incidence of blood in her stool became more frequent in spite of the "kidney" prescription diet. By the summer of 1996, she ceased using the litter box and soiled the floor nearby; always bloody diarrhoea and always crying while she strained to evacuate her bowels. One day when Princess was resting on George's lap she "looked" at him while uttering a most mournful cry. To this day, George believes she was pleading with him, "Help me. I can bear this pain no longer!"

When she came into our lives in October 1994, her age was estimated between four to six years but our current vet disagreed telling us that chronic kidney problems such as hers are very rare in cats under ten years of age. We asked if the starvation she had endured could have hastened her kidneys' malfunction: he did not think so. We had to accept then that Princess was likely much older than previously thought. Even during our many female discussions, Princess, mysterious lady that she was, never revealed her age.

Given her overall physical condition, one that would continue to deteriorate and cause her greater suffering, we made the decision to release our Princess into her next life. In our presence she was put to sleep on November 28, 1996. An amazing loveable, loving cat, tough and tenacious Princess joined our lives for a brief two year period. We will remember her as, "Princess; The Cat who came in from the cold".

Solomon's Story

Our gentle blue eyed king.
Courtly thoroughbred with manners galore,
Solomon so discreet and courteous
all three felines do adore.

Acknowledged patriarch with all three,
only one little flaw; a cowardly fighter is he.
Preferring to beat up a smaller,
sleek and slim little she.

Poor blind Princess seemed so lonely without Dickens who died a few months ago. She walked around searching and crying mournfully. Indeed, being blind, there is very little to interest or stimulate her. We felt the obvious answer was a new feline companion.

My preferred companion for Princess was a mature docile female. In my mind, I could already see Princess and her new friend: two mature ladies, napping companionably on the back of our couch, side by side in the afternoon warmed by the sun filtering through the pale sheers hanging in our front window. A calm contented pair of feline friends exchanging thoughts and opinions about life's trials and tribulations.

Preferably for me, this new feline would be long-haired regardless of the extra work involved. George's only preference was that the new cat be a clown like Dickens who was a Himalayan. I agreed instantly about the breed. But George also felt we should get a kitten, not an adult, and several of our friends agreed with him. They felt, a kitten would bond much more easily to Princess than another adult. Also a male, not another female, was thought to be the better choice for our Princess. I didn't think Princess could stand the business of a kitten but I was outnumbered. Those wiser than I, in the ways of the feline world, suggested that Princess, as the older experienced cat, would soon put a kitten in his place! I agreed.

Of course, once the decision was made, I couldn't wait! I was already retired but George had a week's holiday early May 1995. If we found one quickly then we would both be at home to ensure the kitten would adapt to its new home and new feline companion, Princess. So, the search for a male Himalayan kitten began with a quick scan through the newspapers. After a few phone calls we found an 8 week old seal point Himalayan male kitten available for adoption in the town of Bobcageon. Eureka! The drive would take us approximately two hours but George, Mom and I were on our way.

The breeder lived on a farm. Inside the farmhouse were breeding Persians and Himalayans, while outside a various assortment of domestic cats, dogs and ponies etc. increased in numbers happily on their own. This lady was an all-round breeder. Never having had any experience with breeders, we rather liked this natural, "laissez-faire" farm!

Inside the farmhouse were many cats: adult breeding cats and younger ones of all ages; all extremely friendly and curious about three people coming into their home. For the younger ones, the curiosity was short-lived as they were much more interested in playing hide and seek with each other. As always, when confronted with numerous kittens, I don't want to make one choice but take all of them! However, we had specifically come for a Himalayan seal point like Dickens.

Our little male seal point, born on March 2, 1995, now 8 weeks old, was ready to leave the roost. I had assumed that "seal point" meant dark brown points with taupe brown body just like Dickens but this little mite barely had brown points and a pale cream body. I didn't believe George when he told me that the colour would take up to two years to develop. Regardless, we were smitten with this pale fluffy little mite regarding us with large round ice-blue eyes.

We saw no purpose in purchasing registry papers for our mite but were provided with the names of his parents and grandparents etc. Once our purchase was concluded, our kitten was prepared for a new chapter in his life. Having lived indoors with an extended family, he had never experienced the great outdoors. Within the space of one hour, he was dewormed, given a quick flea bath in the bathroom sink, blown dry and taken by strangers outside and into a noisy car for a long drive. So much handling! Such a frightening experience, all in one day!

During the ride to our home, we discussed a name for our new Himalayan feline and agreed upon "Solomon" which had a majestic ring and which, we felt, was a suitable match to the name Princess, our rescued blind stray cat. We accepted that it would require a few years before Solomon's deeds matched those of his namesake, the wise and noble king of biblical fame.

Inside our car, Solomon would not enter the carrier we had prepared especially for this journey to his new home. Instead, shivering and meaowing pitifully, he crawled from my lap up to my shoulder, around my neck and back down again. Understandably, Solomon was most anxious and scared of noises and sights whizzing by as we drove. This two hour drive must have seemed eternally long for poor little Solomon. Most likely, he felt "catnapped" as Dickens had so many years ago.

When introducing new cats to each other, books advised separation until each is familiar with the other's scent. Even if we hadn't read this advice, we would have separated the two cats because we were worried that if Princess did not accept Solomon, blind or not, she could certainly seriously hurt him. Therefore, a separate nursery for Solomon in the spare bedroom seemed a practical solution, at least at night, when we were unable to oversee the wanderings of our two felines.

Dickens' old wicker basket, cleaned and lined with a woollen sweater, became Solomon's new nest. Inside, we also placed a few soft toys, which at that time were bigger than him. We wanted to make his nest warm and cozy because we knew he would be alone and lonely on his own for the first time ever during his first night in his new home.

In his nursery, we placed a small shallow pan for a litter box. Solomon immediately used his litter box and made a big production of digging, positioning properly and covering up: the finished mound of litter was taller than him! What I scooped out from inside this huge mound was a tiny hazelnut sized pee-ball! Well, our little mite was certainly very neat and thorough! The presence of food and natural curiosity soon dispelled initial fear and caution and soon, he was eating, investigating and playing. We felt relieved.

On the following day, we heard Solomon sneezing and noticed that his eye-rims were red and running. We also noticed something else that we had not at the breeder's, a bald spot, dark and crusty about an inch long, on his tail near his body. Only enthusiastic amateurs such as us would have missed something so obvious! At the first opportunity Monday morning, we presented Solomon to our veterinarian who confirmed, he had an eye infection, a cold and, last but not least, ringworm! Not only had this nasty condition denuded a portion of his tail but also portions of his upper front leg and rear hock. We went home with medication for all three conditions.

Solomon did not seem to suffer from the usual itching of ringworm but within three weeks after his arrival in May 1995, I was scratching, George was scratching and Princess was scratching: ringworm had found another three hosts. All four of us were now on prescription medication for one month. We wondered about Solomon's breeder; surely many of her other animals were also suffering from ringworm and furthermore, surely she must have been aware? While it's true that all her animals were socially very well adapted, we felt that if she was unaware then education was definitely needed.

Nevertheless, our "Mighty Meaow" as Solomon was affectionately dubbed, was an adorable champagne coloured bit of fluff, though I still doubt he is a true sealpoint. It appears from reading material that he might be a seal lynx point with faint mackerel stripes on his front legs. George assures me that the colour will develop over the next two years but I remain doubtful.

Thank goodness, the necessity of a separate nursery did not remain long. Poor Solomon cried at night because he was lonely yet we did not dare leave the door open. However, it soon became obvious to us that Solomon, being sighted and very fast, had the advantage over sightless Princess who simply could not move fast enough. So, the nursery was disbanded within a few days after which Solomon discovered where we and Princess slept at night, on a heated waterbed. Like Princess, he also liked the heat and warmth of company. Consequently, we shared our bed with two cats and, if lucky, we managed to find room for ourselves somewhere between or around them!

Solomon and Princess have an interesting relationship. It's true that Solomon bonded quickly to Princess and I believe that he saw mature Princess as a mother figure. When she eats, he lies close by watching her until she is finished. When she sleeps, he curls up as close by as possible. Adoring Princess, Solomon followed her everywhere and tried all the tricks he could think of to catch her attention or entice her to play. But sadly, Princess remained totally uninterested and would not succumb to any of Solomon's friendly overtures. She rebuffed all attempts at play or close proximity by spitting, snarling, growling or swatting Solomon. Her bonding only reached the level of tolerance but no further. Most likely as I had originally feared, she was just too old for his rambunctiousness.

Nevertheless, his efforts of friendship continued, changing his tactics as he grew. He made himself a perfect nuisance: always sitting in her path causing her to trip over him; sitting near the tip of her tail, he plays with it while she is eating. When Princess approaches her basket, he jumps in ahead of her causing her to trip over him as she climbs in. When she walks over to the couch for a nap, he jumps on the couch first and playfully swats her head or her back as she tries to find another rest-spot. If she heads for the litter box, he quickly jumps in ahead of her thwarting her needy goal. Seemingly undeterred by Princess' rebuffs, Solomon continued with his playfulness: we also dubbed him "Solomon, The Perfect Nuisance".

For his outside escapades, we purchased a very handsome cobalt blue harness and leash, hoping he would accept such an arrangement as Princess did. However, for Princess a leash was literally a lifeline which she gladly accepted, but for Solomon such was not the case. It was a disaster when trying to take him for a walk. He balked, I tugged; he ran, I ran after him. We weren't ready to let him go outside on his own so we persisted, resulting with frustration and without success. We finally gave up on his leash. Luckily for us, as a kitten, he was quite content to stay close to home.

As he learned to jump and climb into everything, he also discovered our dripping tap in the bathroom sink. Being unable to catch the elusive drip was a continued source of fascination, good for hours of entertainment. Solomon tried a few times to climb onto our sheer curtains and an artificial tree located in our living room; he was deterred by my loud and severe, "NO!" to which he eventually listened. Some time ago, George had caught a lake trout that was twice as long as Solomon. Even so, this "giant" fish piqued Solomon's interest. He enjoyed a tidbit of braised laketrout.

During his first veterinarian visit, on May 4, 1995, Solomon, the "Mighty Meaow" weighed only 2.3 pounds but by August of 1995, he weighed a rotund 7.8 pounds; an eating machine whose weight would soon match that of Princess whose weight was 9 pounds. The veterinarian estimated Solomon would reach 15 pounds by maturity. It's hard to imagine that this little fluffball clown will ever become MATURE!

Of course, maturity eventually did arrive. When Solomon reached the equivalent of feline puberty, the male characteristics, in "point" colour, became noticeable, coincident with his more assertive behaviour. Since we were not interested in breeding King Solomon or adding to the community's feral feline population, the time had arrived for a serious visit to our veterinarian in September 1995. This routine operation was successful and before long, our "Solly" was as playful as ever.

Through Princess, who was chronically itchy, we discovered in February 1996, that ringworm, introduced almost one year ago by Solomon, had never actually been cured. Hair samples currently taken from both cats tested positive to this awful condition. Our new veterinarian, being very thorough, offered a literal solution. We were to bathe both cats every week for six weeks with a special medicated shampoo and our house was to be thoroughly sprayed! Six weeks later another hair sample would be tested to ensure that both cats were cured of ringworm.

To our surprise, Solomon who is generally amenable to any handling struggled constantly during his weekly baths. The Himalayan fur is fine, long and dense taking hours to dry even after using numerous towels and a hair dryer. During bath "nights" the heat was usually turned up several degrees for the comfort of our felines. Poor Solomon, not only was his dignity ruffled every week but his lovely champagne coloured fur took on a decidedly ugly yellowish/green tone of colour. Nevertheless, these baths finally cured both cats.

Finally in the summer of 1996 Solomon found a true friend in Nutmeg, one of the two stray female kittens we decided to keep. Solomon was the object of Nutmeg's instant hero worship. She followed him everywhere, played with him and curled up with him. Nutmeg and her sister, Flash Gray-Spot,

61

scavenged food from Solomon's bowl constantly and he, always, moved aside to accommodate them. Soon enough, we realized Solomon was getting very little to eat. Perhaps he has never been hungry enough to fight for his food but I prefer to think of him as a gentlemanly thoroughbred who does not deny his thieving alleycat ladies! The solution was to feed Solomon separately in another room with the door closed; his own private dining room.

Unlike the two sisters who like to be petted anywhere, anytime, Solomon prefers to receive cuddling in private. Truly! He will not sit on our laps within sight of the two sisters. Perhaps he considers such behaviour as un-patriarchal. When he is in a mushy mood, he usually lures George downstairs with a distinct meaow to an area in the backroom where we have odd bits of furniture including chairs. Leading George to one chair, he looks at George pleadingly while his glorious tail is straight up and wafting gently back and forth. George may then pick him up, set him upon his lap and once Solomon settles comfortably, a soft, rumbling purr can only be felt but not heard. Once such a "mushy" session is concluded, Solomon heads upstairs again and immediately proceeds to beat-up Nutmeg. I wonder if Solomon feels he has to counteract his mushy behaviour, even if it was in total privacy, with a reassertion of his dominance.

Solomon acquired another friend the following year in November 1997. Smudge, who was a brother to Nutmeg and Flash Gray-Spot, was truly an outdoor cat. He was coaxed inside to recuperate from an injury following an attack by an older resident tomcat. I believe Solomon sensed that Smudge's confidence was at an all-time low and needed companionship. Good old "Solly" befriended Smudge and very soon, much to Nutmeg's chagrin, the two males were playing and sleeping together.

The play between the two males generally lasted only a minute or two because Smudge, being an in-tact, outdoor cat who had experienced several encounters with other stray territorial males, was more aggressive and powerful than gentlemanly Solomon. Smudge's "play" was decidedly rougher than what Solomon had previously exercised with dainty little Nutmeg. After a minute of "play" with Smudge, Solomon usually ran away leaving his new pal with a rather bewildered expression as if to say; "Hey pal, this was just getting to be fun; come on back!"

Gentleman and patriarch Solomon divides his time fairly between the two sisters and their brother. Nutmeg and Smudge obviously enjoy their playtime with Solomon but not so with Flash Gray-Spot. She seems to interpret any attempt of Solomon's to "play" as a genuine attack and reacts in kind. Perhaps "Flashie" is reminded of the two attacks she suffered as a youngster and is just unable to relate. However, all three acknowledge Solomon as their patriarch and regularly present their heads to him for a subservient little lick. Solomon always obliges but sometimes a little devil in him prompts him to deliver a swat after the last little lick, especially with Flashie, as if to say, "So, there! I'm the Boss and don't you forget it!"

I can always count on Solomon to keep me company when I have a nap. As soon as I lie down, Solomon joins me within a minute, curling up against my shoulder. Nutmeg, who doesn't like to share Solomon with anyone, will join the two of us. She does not curl up gently like Solomon but walks up and down my chest and stomach, kneading all the while, before settling down upon my chest purring in comfort. Flashie also likes to join us and will settle nearby but her presence causes tension between the two sisters. A hissing session begins and stops only when there is a wide separation between them. Such a relaxing afternoon nap!

Solomon is an indifferent eater, eating only to live. He never screams for food like the two sisters and only if he is truly very, very hungry, will he softly approach me and utter a discreet pleading meaow. As I get up, he will lead me to the kitchen and wait patiently underneath the table for me to prepare him a little dish. Once the dish is brought to his private dining salon and placed on the floor, he always sniffs cautiously first, as if to make certain it is "dead", then walks around me from left to right before settling down to eat. This routine never varied. I leave him to eat in peace and close the door. Another discreet meaow will let me know he has had enough, thank you very kindly. When I open the door to let him out, the two sisters run into the room to see if anything worthwhile is left. There usually is.

Although his behaviour seemed normal to us, we knew he had eaten very little during the week before Christmas 2001. We assumed it was time for another hairball treatment. However on December 26, 2001, Solomon hadn't eaten anything for twenty-four hours and had slept continuously. This was most unusual; we didn't like his lethargy and took him to the Emergency Clinic where it was determined that his temperature was very high and white blood cell count extremely low. We learned that unusually warm ears are a clear sign of increased temperature and indeed they felt very warm and looked redder than the usual skin colour. Solomon was placed on intravenous and antibiotics.

An infection, but what was its source? His kidneys were ruled out as the source because he did not vomit food that was given. Unfortunately the few basic blood tests taken did not determine the source of infection. He stayed overnight but on the following day, we were to bring him to our own veterinarian for further blood tests which would be sent to an outside lab for analysis and, hopefully, determine the source of his infection. It was suggested that Solomon might have contracted one of the feline diseases for which there is no inoculation! We were anxious despite believing that doctors know everything. We had a sleepless night.

Further blood tests negated all possible feline diseases however his white blood cell count was still decreasing and his temperature remained dangerously high. We thought that this might be the end of our Solomon but our veterinarian asked for one more day to test bacteria in Solomon's urine which he noticed was abnormally yellow! Indeed, Solomon had jaundice; the source of the infection was his liver but the cause of his infection remains unknown.

In one of my "natural cat" books, I came across a fascinating bit of information possibly relative to Solomon's bout of jaundice. It was stated that severe flea infestations or ringworm may be indicative of liver problems! We know that Solomon was infected with a stubborn case of ringworm when first adopted. Was it possible that his liver was genetically weak?

Our veterinarian told us that Solomon required force-feeding to reactivate his liver function. Miraculously by Saturday morning his body, at last, started to fight off the infection successfully. After many days, his fever was gone and his temperature was normal. His ears no long felt extraordinarily warm and appeared normal in colour and his white blood cell count was increasing and so, we were allowed to bring him home. We were instructed to keep him inside until he was stronger and, if necessary, to continue force-feeding him four times daily until his own appetite returned. Several cans of "Liver Diet" were provided but we were also told to let him eat whatever he fancied as long as he ate; his liver must be forced to function normally again.

Though weak from having lost a lot of weight, we were delighted to see his keen interest in everything when he came home including wanting to go outside! He kept his distance from Nutmeg letting us know that all was not yet entirely normal. Interestingly the two sisters did not go near him either. Did they keep their distance to allow him time to heal or did they instinctively fear illness?

We discovered that force-feeding with a syringe was not only a struggle, but ineffectual. This messy method took too long and either the syringe squirted too much or became plugged. The simple "food-on-the-finger, open mouth & insert" technique worked best for us. Not that Solomon opened his mouth willingly but neither did he struggle. No doubt, a warm soft finger felt more comfortable than the sharp edges of a plastic syringe. After two days of force-feeding, I tried to entice him to eat on his own which he did, and any leftovers were inserted via a finger into his mouth. After another day he ate everything himself. Thankfully, force-feeding was no longer required. We thought he might enjoy some special treats and offered enriched chicken broth, which was eagerly lapped up, as were small pieces of poached sole. His appetite steadily increased to catch up for lost meals.

Although desperate to explore the outside, we kept Solomon inside especially because the weather had turned very cold. Another day when it was slightly warmer and sunny, I put on his cobalt blue harness and took him for a very short walk outside. His natural curiosity prompted him to search everywhere but after only a minute or two I could feel the leash tremble constantly. Whether he was excited or shivering I did not know, but regardless, I brought him indoors immediately. Again, the following day he cried wanting to go outdoors. This time we covered him with a mohair scarf but again, as soon as the cold air hit his lungs he started shivering. After this experience, we kept him inside no matter how much he pleaded with us. He sneezed a few times the following day but thank goodness a full blown cold did not develop and I realized we had been foolish to let him go outside.

After three weeks, he and Nutmeg had resumed their daily ritual of sleeping together and play-fighting. Flashie too, received attempts at play-fighting from Solomon with the usual results. Two months later, his coat looks wonderful and he has gained weight. With his strength regained, he again enjoys prowling around his territory outside. Our Solomon is his amusing, playful mushy self again and everything is back to normal. We want our Solomon around for every one of his remaining eight lives!

While Solomon's ancient ancestors were vigorous outdoor hunters, he and his modern forebears have adapted their hunting skills to the indoors. Following instinct but without the benefit of maternal teachings, Solomon has developed a unique hunting technique. Late one evening, a time when feline hunting instincts reach a peak, we heard "Solly" cry the most peculiar muffled howl. Sounding as though he was choking or in pain, we ran to find out what was wrong. He came up the stairs clutching something in his mouth and was meaowing at the same time resulting in this alarming sound.

Once he reached the kitchen, he dropped his "catch" on the kitchen floor for inspection. We concluded that Solomon had been "hunting" downstairs, "killed" successfully and was "bringing home the bacon", so to speak, alerting the females of his pride that they might wish to enjoy the fruits of his endeavours. Both girls did come to see what all the fuss was about. Nutmeg, who had become a skilled outdoor huntress, was unimpressed while Flash, who is not a huntress, was nevertheless baffled. How were they expected to eat a used crumpled tissue that was not meat? Undeterred, Solomon continues to hunt and we agree that his self-taught skills are politically correct!

This was the first time that we witnessed Solomon's remarkable hunting technique. Previously, periodically when we arose in the morning, we found a trail of used tissues on the floor leading to an overthrown wastebasket in the downstairs bathroom and wondered who had created this mess. Now we knew.

Sometimes his howling is a signal that he is desperate for play. Howling, he will carry a toy ball and drop it nearby and we know it is time for a game of throw and catch. Solomon is a very good basketball player, jumping straight up at least one and a half feet in the air; he will catch the ball in mid-air and then drop it immediately. While he does the catching, I do the tossing and retrieving but we both enjoy the exercise.

Just as Solomon had recovered from his liver infection, disaster struck again on February 22nd. Normally, he went outside just after his dinner and in the meantime, we would have ours. After which, he is waiting at the patio door to be let inside. As I opened the door Solomon came inside limping, blood dripping from his nose and mouth. His breathing sounded harsh and laboured as though the airway was blocked. Oh no, what happened now!

Within minutes we were on our way to the Emergency Clinic. We were told that the noisy breathing originated from having to breathe through his mouth rather than his nose but he was not choking because his tongue was pink. An examination of his mouth revealed that the left incisor was missing. The right side of his lower jaw was slack indicating that it was dislocated. We found out that a cat's lower jaw actually consists of two parts that are hinged together by tissue similar to cartilage. Solomon's cartilage was broken leaving the two halves unhinged. Poor Solly was unable to close or use his mouth.

Palpation indicated a problem with the right shoulder which was swollen and, obviously, sore to touch. An X-ray would determine the exact problem with his shoulder. If it was broken, a trip to Guelph might be necessary to set it properly. His nails were not shredded as is often the case in a car accident. Externally, the rest of him appeared to be all right. During his overnight stay, X-rays and blood tests etc. would be taken and he would receive a morphine patch to control pain as well as an intravenous antibiotic to fight infection. As his injuries did not appear life-threatening, we were asked to transport him to our own veterinarian's office early the next day on Friday morning. A full report, including results of all tests would be faxed to our vet.

Leaving our Solomon in good hands, we drove home and speculated about the cause of his injuries. If he had not been hit by a car then what sort of blunt trauma had taken place? We have never seen Solomon climb into a tree higher than four feet off the ground, so a fall could not possibly have caused his wounds. Solomon is shy with strangers and will run away so surely his injuries weren't caused by a monstrous human? What else could have caused his injuries?

At 7:30AM Friday morning we transported Solomon from the Emergency Clinic to our own veterinarian's office where his dislocated jaw was "popped" back into place and the broken bottom jaw halves wired together. Friday evening we transported Solomon back to the Emergency Clinic for monitoring purposes, until Saturday evening when we brought him home. His jaw would take a minimum of three weeks to heal during which period if he would not eat or drink on his own then he must be force-fed.

X-rays revealed that his shoulder was fractured but not broken, and this would require approximately six weeks to heal provided he was prevented from jumping during this period. Keeping Solomon immobile for six weeks; well, this would be a challenge for us but we would succeed!

In preparation for Solly's enforced immobilization, George constructed a huge lid from fence wire which measured three by four feet and placed it on our dining table. Inside this enclosure we placed bedding, water bowl and litter box: it was high off the ground and offered a fine vantage point. Confined inside, we thought Solomon would be comfortable while recuperating. Once home, Solomon looked around in his new surrounding then fell asleep and continued to sleep for three days almost around the clock. Waking up only once or twice to eat on his own (force-feeding was unnecessary; hallelujah), drink and use the litter box. He had no energy for anything else but sleep, that most miraculous healer of all.

A liquid antibiotic had to be administered twice a day. Four times every day, an antibiotic ointment was dabbed underneath his chin to prevent skin from growing over the wire holding his jaw together. Solomon was very good about allowing us to handle him although he would rather have done without our attention. Yes Sir!

On the fourth day of confinement, he began to complain loudly. We felt this was a positive sign of healing. We removed him from his enclosure and placed him on the floor. He limped towards the back patio door waiting to be let out! Absolutely not! Solomon had to be satisfied with just looking outside; he was certainly very animated with all that he saw. We followed him around as he "checked out" other parts of the house ensuring he did not jump but remained on the ground.

After one week, he began to spend long periods grooming himself again and we believe all is on the mend at last. At this stage, Solomon vocalized his displeasure with being enclosed again for the night. George and I groaned because five more weeks were ahead and each day he vocalized louder against his enforced confinement.

Our veterinarian believes his injuries are entirely consistent with being hit by a car. At the time of the accident, it was dusk to dark and it is possible Solomon was blinded by car lights. We don't believe the accident happened far away, perhaps in a driveway where the speed of the car was just enough to knock him off his feet. Now, whenever Solomon hears the engine of a car, he runs to the backdoor desperately wanting inside. His reaction is proof that indeed he was hit by a car.

Solly's seventh birthday on March 2, 2002 was spent recuperating in a giant cage. He has used up two of his nine lives. Having only seven left, we would have to be very careful with him, no more wandering around on his own outside in the dark. He would have to accept his harness plus leash now or become an indoor cat. We know he will not like such an arrangement but it is safer. I have always felt that keeping cats confined to the indoors was unnatural, and it is, but I accept the wisdom of it now.

Six weeks later, his shoulder had healed and he was "released" from his cage. Solomon must have felt well, because the usual play-fights with Nutmeg resumed and even Flashie was enticed into a vigorous play-fight as well. One week later, under light anaesthesia, the wire holding his lower jaw together was removed. Once home, he was in a rare mood; not groggy as we had anticipated but ready to eat and play. We concluded Solomon was very relieved to be wireless once again and seemed to be ready to take on his feline world as before. He also wants to go outside; oh, oh!

At seven years of age, our "mature" Solly has attained the full colour spectrum dictated by his noble genes, exactly as George had predicted. How could I have ever doubted the wisdom of my husband's words? Over the years, Solomon's colour points have deepened to a charcoal brown covering most of his face, ears, legs and tail. As an immature youngster, the fur on his body was an even pale cream colour but as he matured a "saddle", the colour of "cafe-au-lait" with auburn tips, developed on his back and sides.

The development of this colouring was so subtle that it became obvious only when comparing photos with a few years in between. We feel that our handsome, benevolent Solomon has lived up to and continues to be worthy of his namesake. Long live our King Solomon!

Kaze Kaiser Dickens

Princess

Princess ignoring Solomon's attempts to play with her

Walking over Nutmeg and Solomon, Princess will reach her spot

Solomon

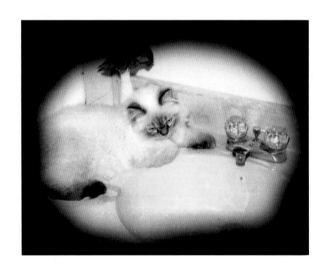

Solomon counting as they fall

Bathing Nutmeg

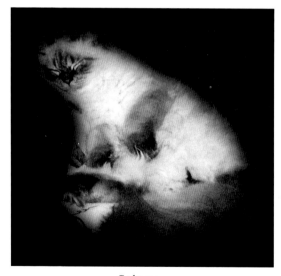

Solomon

Charcoal, Cinnamon, Liquorice and Old Warrior

Old Warrior

Flash Gray-Spot

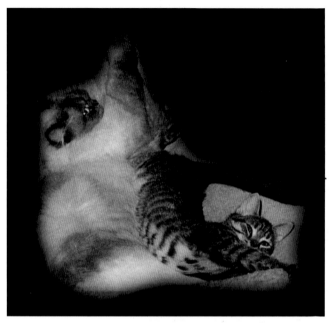

Nutmeg

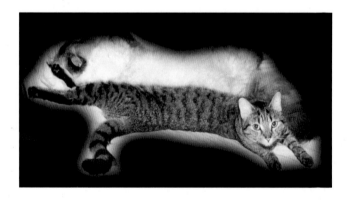

Smudge

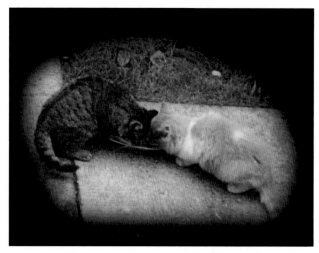

Outdoor group; Young Warrior and Smudge with short tails

Indoor group; Flash Gray-Spot and Nutmeg with longer tails.

Best pals Smudge and Solomon

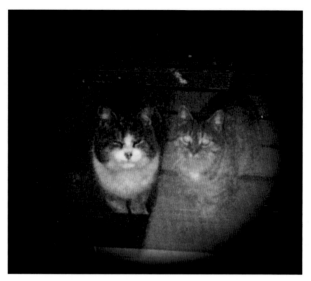

Cinnamon with Scruffy; her champion at last

Cinnamon

Our blind cat, Princess and I were taking our usual after dinner walk; around the house, down the driveway, then a few houses west along Francesca Drive, across the street and then eastwards back home; a large rectangle approximately the size of a half block.

In the first westward stretch, I saw a little black animal dart from the grassy yard and into the woodpile against the side of the house three doors away from ours. My eyes seemed to be playing tricks as I could not see what had darted into the woodpile. The animal seemed too small for a squirrel and since it was still daylight, it wasn't likely to be a skunk. It wasn't a bird. What was it then?

Intrigued, I stood still, waited and watched. There it was again, this time my eyes recognized its shape as that of a tiny black kitten! I stood watching its playful antics when its grey and white litter mate appeared. Then a third litter mate cautiously appeared, also black but fluffier. The first black kitten seemed the most adventurous, while its litter mates were more cautious. From their size, they surely couldn't be older than about four weeks. Is there anything cuter than playful young kittens?

Finally I noticed an adult cat sitting on top of the woodpile. Obviously the mother, she was a well camouflaged dainty cat. A short-haired, black and gold mackerel striped tabby. Mother kept a very watchful eye on her litter and on me! Every time I tried to get closer, all three kittens darted into various crevices of the woodpile. She had trained her litter well; in case of danger, run to safety. At the same time, I guess to divert my attention; Mother ran away in a different direction.

It was March 1995, blustery winds and typically cold. In my mind, nary a hint of spring was in the air. Yet the days were brighter and birds were flying hither and thither, full of anticipation: their seasonal clocks being much more accurate than mine. And since Mother had given birth, surely spring was not far away. But for now, the days and nights were still cold with occasional frost.

I simply had to tell George about this discovery so close to home. Cutting short her walk, poor Princess was raced unceremoniously back home. George came outside with me to have a look. Our next door neighbour had just then stepped outside for a breath of fresh air and, knowing that she was also a cat lover, I excitedly told her what I had seen. The three of us walked to within forty feet of the woodpile site and there we stood, waited and watched. Soon we were rewarded with a display of playful antics by these kittens while Mother kept a wary eye.

Of course, we were immediately concerned about food and the cold. There wasn't much we could do about the cold but we could help feed these kittens to develop a layer of fat to ward off the cold. We flew back home; one would get a plate of kitten food and the other would get a dish of water. After consulting with the owner of the house on whose property the woodpile stood, we obtained his permission to place food/water dishes by his woodpile. There at the entrance of one of the larger crevices we noticed a fresh kill, presumably deposited by Mother to entice her kittens' interest in meat.

Mother was obviously a good provider but we felt we could help her somewhat by leaving food on a regular basis, at least until the warmer weather arrived. We had visions of these little mites starving to death; now that we knew of their existence, we could not let that happen. A regular system of feeding was established and soon these little kittens gobbled up every morsel left for them.

It was wonderful to see these little ones growing and becoming more playful and interested in their surroundings. As the weeks went by, they ventured a little beyond the woodpile but generally at the first hint of danger such as the presence of a human, there was a very quick dash by the kittens back to their woodpile.

About one month later, I heard a tiny meow coming from the wall of the house to the west of ours. When I went over to have a look, I saw the short-haired black kitten huddled against the wall and meowing pitifully. Had it wandered too far away on its own or had Mother placed it there in an effort to teach her little adventurous kitten independence? Regardless of how it got there, it certainly seemed lost and was in distress now.

George came over, knelt down and gently picked up the black kitten cradling it in his hands against his down filled parka where it started to purr, enjoying the warmth. After stroking and cuddling this little one, we decided "Liquorice" would be an appropriate name for this supple short-haired black kitten. George took Liquorice back to the woodpile, where it quickly disappeared into one of the crevices.

As the weeks went by, the kittens grew and became round little roly-poly fluffballs. Their play took them farther afield and soon we saw them running into and around the bushes in our gardens. At this point, I thought I might be able to slowly move the feeding dishes closer to our backyard. Within one week, the family appeared in our backyard for breakfast and dinner. Hesitantly mind you, but there they were.

The "family" at this time consisted of two black kittens and Mother. The third kitten hadn't been seen for weeks; we did not know what had happened. We hoped it had found a kind owner. I mentioned earlier that the black short-haired kitten had been named Liquorice. Its long-haired litter mate was named Charcoal and Mother, due to her colouring, was named Cinnamon.

The feedings were regular and plentiful. Fresh water too, was always available. It didn't take Liquorice and Charcoal too long to become used to my presence, although Charcoal was more nervous. Liquorice was the bolder of the two kittens, and assumed to be male while Charcoal, exhibiting the same reserved skittish behaviour as Cinnamon, was assumed to be female. Cinnamon did not let down her guard in spite of this new found food bonanza and continued her watchfulness just like she had on the first day. We speculated that, due to her behaviour which never changed, Cinnamon was either a truly feral cat, or an abused, abandoned one.

Word of our feedings must have been communicated in feline fashion because within a few days Father showed up too! Father must have been a handsome specimen of a DSH striped tabby as a young lad, long before continued territorial wars altered his appearance permanently. Alas, he was now minus one ear with half the other one gone too. He limped not using his left front paw; perhaps another permanent war wound. Powerful chest, shoulders and neck muscles gave him a formidable appearance: an "Old Warrior" both in looks and, apparently, in deeds.

Yet "Old Warrior" was a softy. He was the first and only cat of that family to allow my touch at which he would purr. Due to his behaviour with me, I believed Old Warrior to be an abandoned stray but not a feral cat. He was also a consummate actor: giving me the most heartbreaking pleading look when waiting for food, the left crippled paw held slightly off the ground. Old Warrior used his limp to perfection for my benefit because when climbing a fence or chasing off some other male, not a trace of the limp was seen.

Our plan, in feeding this family of four, was to catch the kittens and find homes for them. Father and Mother, if caught, would be neutered and spayed and released. We were prepared to feed them indefinitely and if they were happy outdoors, then so be it. Obviously they had found hiding spots which kept them dry and relatively warm. If necessary, as he had done for Princess, George would design an outdoor heated "cat house" for Cinnamon and Old Warrior. A great deal of patience was necessary to affect our plan.

In the meantime, we were able to view the private lives of our cat family. Initially, the kittens were allowed to eat first followed by Mother and Father, but as they grew older, this order of feeding was reversed: Mother first, then Father and last the kittens. The pecking order between the kittens was Liquorice first then Charcoal.

Hissing, spitting, snarling with the occasional swat kept everyone in their respective place and order. As Liquorice grew into a boisterous young lad, he was regularly chastised by Old Warrior. For instance if Liquorice did not await his turn at feeding time, Old Warrior would literally straddle his little body, grab him by the scruff of the neck and growl softly until Liquorice got the message. As naughty as Liquorice was, Charcoal was the opposite, always a good little girl. I never observed Old Warrior chastise Charcoal.

Cinnamon and Old Warrior were a devoted pair. We saw much mutual grooming; though, if Old Warrior's grooming did not live up to Cinnamon's expectation, she swatted him with vigour. We often observed the pair curled up together in the sun or sauntering off together into the sunset after dinner for some private time together leaving their kittens behind. Somehow the kittens knew when to stay behind. It was fascinating to see the adults trotting off together while the kittens watched. Cinnamon was "Salome" to Old Warrior's "Herod".

Eventually when the two kittens were about eight weeks old, we enticed them into a carrier with food. I then brought them to the local Humane Society hoping that this organisation, with their vast animal experience, would be able to tame two well-fed, handsome, albeit wild kittens and put them up for adoption.

The handler caught Liquorice and removed him from the carrier for an examination without a problem: everything was proceeding as I had hoped. In the next second, my hopes were dashed as Charcoal escaped through the carrier's open door and into the reception room. Prior to this occasion, she had never been confined inside a carrier, never mind a building and the poor kitten was terrified. She ran against walls and windows; she was absolutely frantic. Since I had never been able to touch her, there was nothing I could do to help calm her down

91

or catch her. The handler eventually managed to corner, catch and confine Charcoal in a small cage but not before the handler was clawed and bitten.

I was told that the possibility of taming a feral kitten older than four weeks is minimal and Charcoal's reaction was considered "normal" by these professionals. I was horrified to learn that these two eight week old kittens would be euthanized immediately because one had bitten the handler. I was stunned.

I wanted to take them home but felt certain they would never, after this harrowing experience, be enticed into a carrier again for the purpose of neutering or spaying in which case they would eventually add to the feral population in our neighbourhood. I felt I had no option but to leave them behind. I had fed them, watched them grow and now had delivered them to their death. I had become their executioner. What a terrible, terrible day, one which I will never forget.

From that experience, I realized that feeding a feral family has consequences. I became resolved to wean Cinnamon and Old Warrior by allotting progressively smaller portions of food as we progressed into the summer months when nature's food would be plentiful. Nature would then take its course. However, I knew this might be a difficult resolution for me to keep because Cinnamon's belly was enlarging again in an age-old cycle. Another litter was on its way due in the fall of 1995. I never caught a glimpse of that litter; perhaps they did not survive or perhaps some kindly soul captured the kittens at the appropriate time.

In spite of my resolve to cease feeding wild cats, I was still doing so in the summer of 1996. Cinnamon had given birth to another litter on July 14, 1996 and I did not have the heart to cut off her easy food supply while she was lactating. This litter became very special in our lives as you will discover in the story entitled, "A Litter of Our Own".

Early that fall I was feeding a total of nine felines twice a day: our own group of five (Princess, Solomon, Lightning,

Nutmeg and Flash Gray-Spot) plus our feral family of four (Cinnamon, Old & Young Warrior and Smudge). A friend, who knew of my love for cats, once told me that she envisioned me eventually living on a farm with countless stray cats. It appears that a part of my friend's prophecy had become a reality.

I must admit that the growing numbers of cats to be fed was becoming a worrisome burden. It seemed, the longer I continued to feed Cinnamon, the larger and healthier her litters became. Generally she had four litters per year; each litter ranging from three to five kittens. At an average of four kittens per litter, I could be responsible for an increase of possibly sixteen cats annually to our local population of feral felines. I did not want that responsibility!

My resolve became firm in the spring of 1997 and, as I had suspected, it was a difficult task: no more food. Old and Young Warriors had disappeared but, as usual, Cinnamon came to our back patio twice a day for many weeks waiting patiently for her food. Each time she waited an hour or more. I found it heartbreaking but felt I must not give in: at last, after a few months, she gave up. The cycle was broken.

However, resourceful cat that she is, Cinnamon did not starve. I discovered that our neighbour, also a cat lover, took over where I left off. Our neighbour captured one of Cinnamon's litter in the summer of 1997; a long-haired tortoiseshell kitten whom she named Zoe. Consequently our neighbour felt so guilty about having "catnapped" one of Cinnamon's kittens that she felt compelled to continue feeding the mother; lucky Cinnamon.

On her way to or from our neighbour's yard, Cinnamon regularly crosses ours, appearing well-fed. She continues to do best what nature intended and that is, of course, to produce litters. Without fail they are beautiful litters. Usually there are four; an orange tabby, a mackerel striped tabby, a long-haired charcoal one and one with mixed colouring; white legs and belly while the upper body is darkly striped. Proud Mother introduces her kittens to the world at large when they are about four weeks old.

With our neighbour, we have managed to capture a few litters and brought them to our Humane Society where they are placed for adoption a few weeks later when they are about six to eight weeks old. Without doubt these adorable kittens will be adopted but I wonder if the adoptive owners ever speculate about their feral mother whom we named "Cinnamon"; wily and resourceful Mother of their darling new kittens.

Allspice & Her Litter

Knowing about my love of cats, my hairdresser, an impeccable source of all local news, told me one day that her neighbour Jane was raising four very young kittens, apparently abandoned by their mother in a nearby backyard. No-one had seen the mother cat around for a day or two and, since Jane's reputation as a knowledgeable "cat person" was well known, those who were concerned about these mewling kittens asked Jane to come and have a look. Guessing that the kittens were perhaps only three to four weeks old and therefore too young to be left on their own, Jane took them home and became their foster mother.

My interest was immediately piqued and I wished aloud to my hairdresser that I could see these little ones. My wish was granted. George and I were invited to Jane's home, only a block away, to meet the rescued litter; two black ones (one long-haired and the other short-haired) and two striped tabbies (one orange and one mackerel). They were indeed very young, their legs just a tad longer than the length of Jane's "shag" carpet. I wondered whether the shag length appeared like a series of high hurdles to the kittens or did it feel pleasant reminding them of Mother washing their tummies?

Jane told us that during their first few days, she had bottle-fed each little kitten four times daily: that is sixteen feedings! Now they had graduated to eating enriched baby Pablum from a plate. Mealtime had arrived during our visit and as four small plates were placed on the floor, four kittens came running and tumbling as fast as their uncoordinated little legs could carry them. Only one kitten had the good manners to eat from the plate but the others thought the Pablum tasted much better if they sat in it! What a sight: four little ones licking and smacking away. It was our task to assist in cleaning up the squiggling kittens afterwards. Hardly a task but more like a labour of love!

Trying to find homes for these kittens, Jane hoped we would take one, perhaps two; however, we could not since we already had Solomon and Princess. In addition to our own cats, we were also feeding a stray couple, Cinnamon and Old Warrior, plus their most recent litter. In total, we were already feeding six cats twice a day: I could not cope with any more. Jane understood. George and I promised Jane that we would spread the word to our friends and co-workers in order to find homes for her adorable kittens. We would keep in touch.

I felt that the kittens were very lucky indeed to have been rescued by such a benevolent soul as Jane. Otherwise, at their tender age they would not have survived the elements on their own. I wondered why they had been abandoned; had the mother died or been frightened away from her very young babies? Would we ever know?

At home on the following day, a new adult cat joined Cinnamon, Old Warrior and their litter for a meal at our home. Strangely, there was no rivalry or altercation between the three adults; in fact the trio seemed very comfortable with each other. Like Cinnamon often did, this new adult stretched luxuriously and rolled enticingly near Old Warrior. Based on this behaviour, I suspected the new cat was female.

Except for the fact that the newcomer had long hair, whereas Cinnamon is short-haired, these two were duplicates of each other; two peas in a pod. I felt certain that the new cat was related to Cinnamon; perhaps a sister and so named her, what else but, Allspice.

I thought such friendly behaviour between two females and one male unusual but then recalled the dynamics in a pride of lions with one supreme male and several females plus their numerous offspring. Perhaps this was a similar relationship: two sisters, Cinnamon and Allspice, and one male. Old Warrior might be crippled and ugly but he managed a harem of two adoring females whose behaviour would have made Jezebel blush!

However, relative to this story, the most interesting aspect about Allspice was that she was lactating yet her kittens were nowhere to be seen. What had happened? Had she abandoned them? So, between our home and Jane's, only a block apart, there was an abandoned litter and a lactating queen minus her litter. Too great a coincidence; surely Allspice was the mother of Jane's kittens?

Based on observation and reasoning I believe I can present a good argument that Allspice is indeed their mother and that Old Warrior is their father. I have already described the "friendly" behaviour observed between Allspice and Old Warrior and therefore accept that he would sire her litters.

Since Allspice and Cinnamon were identical in colouring, it seems reasonable to me that the colouring of a litter between each female and Old Warrior would be similar as well. Again, from observation, I can confirm that the colouring of Jane's kittens was very similar to the kittens produced by Cinnamon at regular intervals with Old Warrior as their sire. Although I cannot provide absolute proof, there is no doubt in my mind that Allspice is the mother of the kittens boarding with Jane and Old Warrior is their sire.

Having solved the mystery about the kittens' lineage, at least in my mind, the remaining puzzle for me was why Allspice had deserted her litter? From a few more conversations, with Jane and my hairdresser, came some interesting information. Deck renovations were apparently in full swing in the yard next to where the kittens were found. The noise of men at work, hammering and sawing every day for eight hours per day must have been extremely frightening as well as distressing for any mother cat nurturing very young kittens.

I believe that Allspice gave birth a few weeks before the deck building project started when her chosen birth spot was peaceful, quiet and hidden from all dangers. Then, when the kittens were a few weeks old, noise of the renovation project shattered the safety, peace and quiet of the nursery area. At that point, being either an inexperienced mother or in extreme distress with the constant racket, Allspice abandoned her litter and joined Cinnamon and Old Warrior at our home.

As suddenly as Allspice appeared, she disappeared about one week later; perhaps coincident with the completion of the deck renovations. I assume she went back to her own territory because we never saw her again. Through Jane's continued efforts, good homes were found for each of the four abandoned kittens: a successful conclusion to an event that could have ended tragically. These are the happy endings I like.

A Litter of Our Own

"Flash Gray-Spot"

Round luminous eyes,
a tiny pink nose, her body white and black
thundering around with all her might:
hoping to find a snack.

Aloof and apart she stays,
except for one chosen moment at the end of all days.
On your lap she stays with adoring eyes pleading
for fifteen minutes of purring and kneading.

"Nutmeg"

Tiny and trim, sleek and slim,
instinctive huntress, seductive temptress,
our Bathsheba.

Solomon encircled by her long beringed tail,
she has no need to waft a gossamer veil,
our Bathsheba.

Ever inquisitive, seldom still,
bewitching daughter of Cinnamon,
our Bathsheba.

After an absence of two days, Cinnamon reappeared looking svelte and most likely ravenously hungry. We knew then that a regular miracle had occurred: a litter had been born, most likely on the first day of her absence, July 14, 1996. We wondered how many kittens were born this time. No doubt, in time we would discover.

As usual, Cinnamon, of no fixed address, devoured her food in haste: her amber eyes darting around searching for possible danger. After feeding her regularly for over a year, we were no closer to being able to touch her than the first time we fed her: the hope of catching, spaying and releasing her would, unfortunately, remain a dream. I have never known a cat as skittish as Cinnamon and wonder if her behaviour was natural or not?

However, by continuing to feed her, she was likely to bring her litter to us when they were about four weeks old. If she did and we could catch them, then our plan was to either find homes for them or bring them to a local shelter. Either way, the kittens would not increase our neighbourhood feral feline population. That was our grand plan.

I was told that feral kittens should be caught preferably when four weeks old, any older and domestication is unlikely. Additionally, after that age they are far too fast; I know. So, we waited; days and weeks went by. At last, about four weeks later, we occasionally heard a kitten meaowing loudly. One evening, I followed the meaowing to its source along the east wall of the next house and there scooped into my hands a very young kitten: I had caught my prize!

"Lightning", a male, was named after the white flash between its eyes up onto his forehead. He was long-haired with white underbelly and legs. On his sides and back was a colour pattern of black and tawny mackerel shading in the shape of a "saddle". His nose and paw pads were a delicate pink while his ears were still folded slightly forward. Lightning was so little and young, yet in the palm of my hand he resisted capture bravely defending himself by growling, hissing and spitting.

Although his spitting, not yet perfected at his tender age, sounded more like a sneeze to me.

Now that I had caught my prize, I wasn't about to let him go, but we hadn't prepared anything for a small kitten either. Because Lightning was wild and likely had fleas and heaven knows what else, we wouldn't bring him inside our home. So, once again, our garage was used as a home for Lightning. A warm bed was quickly made in the corner of a huge box. This would have to do until we could think of a better arrangement the next day.

Being so young, he would have to be kept very warm and also be fed a special diet close to Mother's milk. From another cat lover and substitute mother-to-kittens, we learned that very young kittens, like human babies, need to be fed every four hours. George and I didn't have any idea how often Lightning should be fed but we began with a schedule of every four hours. Beginning that evening, every four hours Lightning was fed an enriched mixture of milk, egg yolk and baby Pablum, setting the alarm for the night feeding at 2 AM. One can only imagine what the neighbours thought if they saw us, clad in housecoats, going outside to the garage with a flashlight in hand in the "wee" hour of the morning!

Not only does a young kitten need to be fed frequently but at that age, so we were told, their bodily functions need to be prompted as well. We simulated Cinnamon's grooming with a warm wet wash cloth which worked very well. Within two days, Lightning was no longer growling etc., but purring and his little ears were now positioned straight up in an alert position. His box in the garage was not large enough to hold him for longer than a day or so. A roomier "home" was needed until a permanent home was found for him.

George had another ingenious idea using three large wire open-ended stacking baskets. Each basket was almost two square feet and stood one foot high. These were inverted on a platform of insulation and connected to each other at their open ends; the connecting area became therefore a triangle which was covered by a piece of gypsum board. Voila, a four room modular townhouse for Lightning. One basket became the bedroom; the second became his bathroom while the third became the playroom. Meals could be served in the three sided room but for the first few days, I preferred to feed Lightning on my lap. He was such a cutie! During sunny days, his multi-roomed modular townhouse was moved outside on the patio deck or on the grass. Lightweight and portable housing...maybe this ought to be patented.

When Solomon, our gentle Himalayan king, came outside, he was very intrigued, his nose working overtime trying to figure out who this newcomer was. It wasn't long before Solomon tried to initiate play via an outstretched paw towards Lightning. True to form, our elderly blind cat, Princess, sniffed, spat and walked away.

Lightning was very playful and curious. I fashioned a tiny harness from string for Lightning. He didn't like this tethering arrangement but we went for our little walks. Along the west wall of our home is a wide rose bed in front of which stretches a stone walkway. When our roses are in bloom, it is a delightful walk full of lovely colour and scent. I took Lightning along this walkway and for some reason, unknown to me, Lightning felt he had to jump from one stepping stone to the other; perhaps the grass blades tickled his tummy. The space between each stone is about four inches; the length of his little body. Though a great jumper, the poor mite must have been exhausted from all that jumping at the end of our walk!

The days took on a regular routine of feeding, bathing sleeping and playing. We soon discovered that Lightning's digestive system was developed enough to forego the 2AM feeding and he could tolerate a bit of soft kitten food in his enriched milk formula. He was growing before our eyes. In the meanwhile I was telling everyone within hearing that a kitten was available for adoption at the end of August when he would be eight weeks old. We also left signs in various places as well.

One week after Lightning was caught, George noticed a small oval shape against the wall of the next house while enjoying his first smoke of the day. As he came closer, he recognized the oval shape as a tiny kitten curled up. Hoping not to be noticed, this kitten didn't move and made no sound. This tactic would have worked in the wild where this kitten's tawny striped colouring would have provided excellent camouflage but not against a red brick wall. George placed this tawny striped "oval" kitten in the palm of his hand, came inside and showed me his prize. This was undoubtedly Cinnamon's kitten, almost a perfect duplicate; what else should she be named but "Nutmeg". Displaying a docile, quiet and dainty demeanour, little Nutmeg is believed to be a female.

While I reintroduced Nutmeg to her brother Lightning, George went outside to finish his cigarette and heard a tiny meaow; following the sound to its source, George scooped up Lightning's twin. The only difference between Lightning and his twin was a grey striped spot in the middle of the latter's white chest: therefore "Flash Gray-Spot" if you please. As far as we could tell Flash Gray-Spot was a female. With Lightning's litter mates catnapped from Mother Cinnamon, the garage nursery now contained three kittens, one brother with two sisters. There was enough room for all three but not for very long. More signs were posted in our vet's office and local stores.

Undoubtedly Cinnamon was their mother and Old Warrior, likely the father of Nutmeg but was he the father of twins Flash Gray-Spot and Lightning? The twins are completely different from Nutmeg. Their body shape is broader and bigger; they are long-haired with white undersides and legs. Their upper back and sides are black with a hint of tawny mackerel striping and a flash of white in the middle of their back. Also the shape of their head is rounder than Nutmeg's. Their citrine coloured eyes are round whereas Nutmeg's are almond shaped.

Another stray male who has been around for a while, is dubbed "Old White Belly" though in truth, I don't know his age. He has the same rounded head, eye colour and white underside but is tawny coloured on the upper side and is short-haired. A third male, possibly intact, is dark and long-haired with occasional tawny colouring. He too has unusual citrine coloured eyes but there is no white anywhere on his body. The twins seem to have features of both males. I have heard that it is possible for a litter to have more than one father but is it possible for one kitten to have the genes of two fathers? Who fathered Lightning and Flash Gray-Spot? I think this is a fascinating mystery!

The daily routine settled into with Lightning, now tripled to include Flash Gray-Spot and Nutmeg; consequently most of my day was enjoyably occupied. For a retiree I was a very busy lady. Feeding took place in the triangle room after which each kitten was bathed; personal grooming and mutual grooming was just beginning. Bathing consisted of a vigorous rubdown with a warm wash cloth followed by drying with another little towel: these actions must have felt similar to Cinnamon's grooming because they always resulted in the most appreciative purring and kneading.

After drying, they were dusted with yeast to discourage as many fleas as possible. Our little litter didn't like the yeast very much but we didn't like their fleas very much either!

Warm summer weeks flew by. Our kittens were growing bigger and stronger. Personalities were developing. Nutmeg remained very docile while Lightning and "Flashie" were more adventurous. Lightning was definitely the more aggressive while Flashie's enterprising curiosity got her into trouble, sometimes with near disastrous results. Soon they would be too big to keep confined in their three room modular house but where could we let them loose yet confined?

We moved our car into the driveway so that our litter could run loose in our garage for an hour in the morning and evening. This seemed to be a good solution until George found Flashie caught in the loops of his fishnet scoop. Struggling desperately to free herself from strangulation, she used one of her nine lives. We didn't want any further mishaps and realized one of us would have to supervise these play sessions. It would only be a few weeks more before we could bring our litter to the vet's office for their first true flea bath after which we could bring them inside our house.

At last, a young fellow answered my advertisement offering free kittens to loving homes. He was searching for a "special" birthday present to give to his mother. Our "price" was right for this young lad. Of the three kittens, he chose Lightning to be his "special" present. His family, which included grandparents, already had a dog and a cat but he thought a kitten was needed to complete his family grouping. He felt certain his mother would agree; it was clear to me that he had given his idea a great deal of thought! Driving him and his "special present" home, I suggested he call me if there was a problem. I did not hear back.

No further inquiries were received about the remaining two kittens however by this time George was very fond of Nutmeg, whom he affectionately still referred to as his "little oval" while I thought Flash Gray-Spot was an adorable long-haired fluffball: as you can probably guess, we kept both. Four (cats) being such a nice even number, don't you think so too?

On my birthday, September 18, 1996, Nutmeg and Flashie received their professional flea bath and graduated from the garage into our home. The vet's office had pronounced the sisters to be in good health and the usual feline inoculations were begun. Jeremy's room became the indoor nursery for a few weeks until Solomon and Princess got used to their new housemates. Solomon liked his two new playmates and was ready to play but Princess did not and, as usual, let them know in no uncertain terms.

Once our litter was given the run of the house, it didn't take long before our bed was usurped by four cats! They would have slept with us at night too except George and I realized there simply wasn't enough room for all of us. It is one thing for cats to sleep all day on top of the covers but at night their kneading on our waterbed was thought to be unwise. George and I had visions of waking up in a pool! Much to our litter's dismay, we closed our door at night. George and I endured a few nights of meaowing, howling and door scratching but soon each found their own special spot. Life went on.

Nutmeg immediately befriended Solomon and their friendship has remained close to this day. They sleep and play together. She is his Bathsheba, a provocative hussy especially when initiating play as she always does. A long slim elegant front leg will brush Solomon's face and the fracas will start. Their play-fights are comical to watch, Nutmeg always flops on the floor thereby gaining the advantage of using four legs. Solomon generally sits and is able to use only one or two front legs during the attack but since his legs are shorter, he has to plan strategically to get close enough for a nip. After a few minutes of being kept at bay by her longer legs, the "fight" becomes mean and Solomon resorts to biting her bum. His nastiness provokes a warning hiss after which Nutmeg walks away until the next time.

Like her mother Cinnamon, Nutmeg has become a skilled huntress preferring to be outside only when it is dark. Very proud of her newly self-taught skills, she brought her first "kill" to me. I was not so pleased and took it away from her. Of course, afterwards whenever she caught a bird or mouse, she brought her "catch" near me, but just out of reach and I was unable to catch Nutmeg. During warm summer nights, she stays outside until the early hours of the morning. Her "croaky" voice, sounding like a foghorn, lets me know she when is ready to come inside which usually happens at 4 AM when dawn is starting to break.

Also like her mother, Nutmeg remains very shy and nervous and runs for cover at the sound of a doorbell or strange voice. Being the most affectionate of our quartet, she loves to be cuddled and groomed rewarding you with vigorous kneading, purring, closed eyes and a steady stream of drool drops. George is the recipient of most of her affections and he gives her cuddle time at least twice daily. If he is sitting on our front couch, she will walk along the backrest, tail held high, and once behind his head, pauses and droops her tail bewitchingly over his hair and face until the tip touches his lips. George is lucky I am not a jealous woman!

Nutmeg is also the most "talkative" of our cats. When lying behind us on the couch in front of the window, she will chatter incessantly for several minutes. I imagine she is telling us what is going on outside, the weather, birds flying by and the postman delivering mail etc. She utters short grumbles, low or high squeaks and other staccato chortles. If I ask her to repeat what she said, she willingly does so!

Although Nutmeg's health is good and her coat very glossy we do have to keep a close eye on her. About two years ago, she had the feline equivalent of an asthma attack. We did not notice anything until it was almost too late. Nutmeg, usually the most active of our cats, sleeps the least and is always busy. We realized, one day, that she had been quite lethargic for a few days and now noticed her sides were vigorously pumping air continuously. Off to our vets who kept her in overnight to stabilize her condition; we now keep medicine available at all times. We have no idea what caused this attack; perhaps some scent or household cleaning spray. I no longer use many sprays and thankfully, we have not had to use any of Nutmeg's reserve medication.

During the long winter months, Nutmeg keeps her skills honed with an inventive game involving our so-called dripless tap in the bathroom. It does drip and Nutmeg is right there with her head turned almost 250 degrees to catch it whenever it should fall. We always know when she has been playing this game; she leaves wet tell-tale footprints all over the vanity! During the night if we are awakened by a heavy thump, we know that Nutmeg has finished playing her favourite game and has jumped to the floor looking for a new game.

Solomon, whom we had dubbed "The Perfect Nuisance" in his youth, undertook to teach Nutmeg everything he knew. He taught her well: always underfoot demanding attention at all times and always chattering. Our dainty little lady is a graduate from the renowned school "**N.U.I.S.A.N.C.E**." short for **N**ever **U**nderestimate the **I**mportance of **S**tealth, **A**ttack, a **N**ap or

Catnap and Eating. The envy of her classmates, Nutmeg graduated with the highest honours and was awarded the title "NUISANCE Supreme". As "NUISANCE Supreme", she has been invited numerous times to lecture as a guest speaker and shares her perfect skills with other keen students: regrettably, for them being a constant nuisance at home leaves her too little time for duties elsewhere!

As Nutmeg was drawn to Solomon, Flash Gray-Spot was drawn to Princess but sadly for Flashie, Princess, as always, rebuffs all attempts at companionship. Flash had to learn life skills without the benefit of a mature feline friend. As a young kitten, Flash remained the more adventurous and used up another two of her nine lives inside our home before she reached maturity. Shortly after the kittens came inside our home, she again nearly strangled herself. This time she had pushed her head through the two rows of plastic cording at the bottom of our vertical blinds and was unable to extricate herself. Twisting and turning frantically, she was literally strangling herself. Thank goodness, George was nearby to see her struggling furiously and managed to cut her loose before it was too late. Another time an involuntary plunge into the cold water of the toilet bowl gave her a terrific scare. Everywhere in our house, we had to remove possible dangers to prevent further mishaps because now, our Flash Gray-Spot has only six lives left!

When Flash was almost a year old, she was attacked by Old White Belly, a tomcat who may or may not have been her father. I heard the screams and went outside to rescue her. Terrified, she came flying inside and ran into the basement where she hid for several hours before I was able to coax her upstairs and eventually outside again. Ever since that traumatic event, she prefers to go outside generally only with us and in the daylight. When George and I are walking around our garden, Flash will accompany us faithfully. Unfortunately Flash does not realize her huge size could be used to great advantage: at heart, she is a dainty lady of loveable proportion with large soft luminous eyes.

Even in adulthood, she has retained the kittenish quality of a tiny high pitched meaow. Her internal clock, as accurate as Greenwich Time, sounds off promptly at designated mealtimes; she always "rings" the first alarm. As we are busy preparing dishes of food for our litter, her meaowing increases in urgency and pitch, reaching a crescendo, until her food bowl is on the ground. In fact, her nose is quite often in the food bowl before it reaches the ground. Judging by her frantic screams, one might conclude that she was cruelly being starved but one look at her roly-poly body will dispel such thoughts.

Food is her passion; she lives to eat. I know that if given the chance, Flash Gray-Spot could and would eat all day long, probably earning her a spot in the Guinness Book of World Records. The only way to ensure she eats only her own diet food is for me to stand guard. Once our quartet is finished, the bowls are gathered and washed. Food cannot be left out for an occasional nibble.

Regardless, it is still a battle to control her weight which is around eighteen pounds. I suspect our vet believes we are over-feeding her but this is not true. Her steady weight gain began after she was spayed. We believe that her metabolism is very slow and wonder if spaying is responsible. I still search for a safe way to satisfy her obsession, other than minimal calories, so that she might be a sleek and svelte lady once more.

As kittens, the sisters were great friends with constant games of chase and play-fights. Now, as adults, any interaction is marked only by hissing, spitting and swatting: friends no more! We believe Flash's passion for food might have caused the sister's permanent estrangement. In 1998 George and I flew to Newfoundland for one week to celebrate the 500th landing anniversary of explorer John Cabot's ship named "Matthew". Unable to find a live-in "cat-sitter", our litter was boarded: Nutmeg and Flash were lodged in one large cage and Solomon in another. Upon returning home from our holiday, we noticed that the two sisters had become arch enemies. What had happened? Knowing Flash as we do, we concluded that she likely ate everything leaving nothing for Nutmeg. After several such days, a ravenous Nutmeg likely fought Flash for a share of food. We believe Nutmeg has never forgiven Flash for such unsisterly behaviour.

Flashie loves to sleep in the sun or in front of the heat register and if she then receives a tummy massage, well then she is in heaven. Her coat, a peculiar mix of coarse and fine long hair, is extremely dense and requires frequent grooming: an activity which she loves; purring and kneading all the while. If a day passes and we have forgotten to pay enough attention to her, Flash will jump into the bathroom sink, which she now fills entirely, and howl until we respond to her call.

As young kittens though, Flash and Nutmeg had a wonderful time in our home as demonstrated by our shredded furniture, rugs and curtains. Neither yelling nor spraying with cold water would deter them from stropping. The two sisters regularly climbed into an artificial tree for a game of chase amongst the branches. Well, what else are trees for, especially in the winter time when you are young, confined to the indoors and have so much energy?

For the first five years of their lives, I did not dare put up a Christmas tree with hundreds of dangling wooden ornaments; such enticement would have been impossible for them to ignore. During Christmas 2000, when they were four and a half years old and a little calmer, I finally dared. My patience was rewarded as our Christmas tree remained, for the most part, untouched for the duration of its display. Our house is not perfect and often I lament the shredded shabbiness of our furniture but then I relent and admit that I would not be without "A Litter of Our Own".

Smudge's Story

Cuddly boy Smudge,
no fighter is he,
preferring to let it be.

When inside the house, he plays with his mouse.
Weather permitting, outside he roams,
chasing all manner of gnomes.

Cuddly as can be,
affectionate, orange and white is he.
Jealous his sisters remain and will not let him be.

During September 1996, Cinnamon came around for her feedings with two more kittens whom I had not seen before. Obviously, these two kittens were siblings of her July 14, 1996 litter, meaning that the total number of kittens born to that litter was five! In early August, we had captured three of her kittens; a male named Lightning, his twin sister Flash Gray-Spot and Nutmeg, another sister as described in "A Litter of Our Own".

Of the two kittens not seen prior to September 1996, one was a short-haired mackerel striped tabby identical to Nutmeg and most likely her twin. Undoubtedly, "Old Warrior", also a mackerel striped tabby, is their father. The new kitten's dominant behaviour surely meant it was male? Along with his personality and compact little body, I foresaw another formidable male just like Old Warrior sometime in the future: this kitten, as a duplicate of his father was named, what else but "Young Warrior".

The second new kitten had an orange smudge on the lower chin and upper right lip and, of course, was named "Smudge". Just like Lightning and Flash Gray-Spot, Smudge had the same round head and large sturdy body and was long-haired. All three had white underbellies and legs but whereas Lightning's and Flashie's mackerel pattern was coloured predominantly black and tawny, Smudge's colouring was orange and pale gold. Except for the colour difference, these three kittens resembled one another in all aspects and I believe them to be triplets but since none bear any resemblance to Old Warrior, I doubt that he is their father but, then who is?

Always around and fighting with Old Warrior over Cinnamon, is another male named Old White Belly. "Old" is a reference to the many battles scars worn by both males but in truth I haven't any idea about either cat's age. However, generally Old White Belly is the loser of these battles. I say "generally" but perhaps not always because Old White Belly, like the triplets, has the same round head and large body shape, white legs and underbelly with dark, beige and tawny mackerel shading on his side, back and tail. Like theirs, his paw pads and nose are pink. Quite possibly, he could be their father except for the fact that, unlike them, he is short-haired. From whom did they inherit the long fur? I think it was their mother, Cinnamon who may have had a recessive long-haired gene because in every one of her previous litters there was always one long-haired kitten.

Oh, oh, oh! Two likely fathers of one litter, that wily Cinnamon; it appears that "Scarlett" would have been a more appropriate name! T.V. soap operas could not compete with the feline going-on in our neighbourhood!

Aside from my fascination with who sired which kitten, Young Warrior and Smudge with motor skills co-ordinated at eight weeks of age were too fast to catch. I wondered if

Cinnamon had purposely kept these two kittens out of our sight, knowing that we had "catnapped" her other three. Impossible to capture, these two kittens would remain "wild", with the exception of receiving regular meals at our home. Any "meals" they killed would be the result of instinct but not because they were hungry.

At mealtimes, Young Warrior ate first swatting Smudge away until he was satisfied. Smudge accepted Young Warrior's dominance and waited patiently. Of course, if Young Warrior had left nothing for Smudge, I refilled the plate ensuring that Smudge ate too! There was no doubt about the hierarchy between these two kittens. And due to Smudge's docile behaviour, we assumed Smudge was female.

Smudge and Young Warrior were adorable. With regular feedings, their bodies developed a protective layer of fat while their fur became thick and dense as the seasons headed towards winter. Surprisingly though, their tails were short compared to those of their indoor sisters, Nutmeg and Flash Gray-Spot whose tails were twice as long. Lightning had been adopted so the length of his tail is unknown but I suspect it is as long as his indoor sisters. I was puzzled by the difference in tail length between indoor and outdoor siblings, but finally concluded that nature knew exactly what it was doing. For the outdoor kittens, nature wisely directed all development towards a thick coat of fur and to their internal organs. A short tail would be a minor, trade-off for winter survival. I felt quite certain that their tails would grow to normal length next summer.

The outdoor cats were fed outside on our backyard patio. Initially Cinnamon ate with her two kittens from one bowl while Old Warrior ate from another. As the kittens grew, Cinnamon left her kittens to share one bowl while she moved to share another with Old Warrior. Feeding the outdoor cats was of great interest to our indoor ones who lined up inside the patio doors to watch the outdoor diners. There didn't seem to be any recognition between indoor and outdoor siblings, so that if they did meet outdoors there was curiosity which quickly turned into hissing and spitting followed by each going their separate ways.

As the colder winter months approached and the kittens were weaned, Cinnamon turned her attentions elsewhere, leaving them on their own for longer periods each time. George again turned his thoughts to protecting Young Warrior and Smudge against winter's frost. From insulation, he built a two-storey house. At the back of the ground floor was an opening, through which the cats accessed their second floor sleeping quarters. That opening also allowed heat from a construction lamp to rise and warm their beds. The second floor was just large enough to accommodate two sleeping cats curled up together.

From their sleeping quarters, they would view the prevailing weather conditions through a tiny window. If weather was viewed to be inclement, then the occupants could choose to remain inside, warm and dry. A fresh bowl of water was inserted through the removable window every day and placed just inside on the second storey. Also positioned inside was a thermometer which registered a mean temperature of 40 degrees Fahrenheit when the outside temperature was well below zero degrees Fahrenheit. Not once did the water bowl freeze during the winter of 1996/97.

Almost immediately, Young Warrior and Smudge took possession of their new quarters. The heat generated by their bodies plus that of the heat lamp caused their little window to be covered with condensation. That winter, weather permitting, we often saw two sleepy heads emerge from their comfy quarters, stretch and yawn and climb up the steps to the patio door waiting to be fed. Pretty lucky wild kittens, wouldn't you agree?

In between mealtimes, inseparable Young Warrior and Smudge played games such as hide and seek amongst the snow banks. Leaping, chasing and pouncing upon one another, they rolled in the snow. If the temperature was above freezing, puddles formed in our driveway initiating another amusing game: catch your reflection, if you can. We saw the kittens standing in puddles of cold water, jump and then watch their own reflection ripple away. Paws reached out into these ripples many times but not once were they able to catch that elusive reflection! What a delight for us to watch.

While we were enchanted with our feral feline friends, our neighbours were not and rumours flew about there being too many wild dirty cats especially one "crippled dirty old male". That description must have meant Old Warrior who indeed did limp. Both he and Young Warrior disappeared in March 1997. I had found these two easy to approach: unfortunately, that may have caused their end. There might also be another explanation for their disappearance and that relates to survival of the fittest. If there is room for only one dominant male in a given territory, it is possible that Old Warrior may finally have died of wounds inflicted by his arch rival, Old White Belly. Old White Belly may also have killed his rival's offspring, Young Warrior. No matter what the scenario, we never saw them again.

Shortly after their disappearance, Cinnamon showed up with Old WhiteBelly, her champion at last. Now pregnant with her first litter of 1997 she had no time at all for Smudge. Cinnamon had taught her daughter everything she knew about survival. The results of her teachings would now be put to the test: Smudge was on her own. Rebuffed by her mother, poor Smudge searched everywhere for her brother, Young Warrior, calling him as she wandered around to all their favourite places. Alone, Smudge seemed lost in the great outdoors though she wisely stayed close to her "larder", our home.

We decided then that we would look after her as our Pet and that meant she would have to be spayed when the time came. In April 1997, she was lured into a cat carrier with food and brought to our vets' office in April 1997. The operation was successful but we were surprised when told that our docile Smudge was not spayed but neutered; "she" was a "he"! Well, it took months before referring to Smudge as a male sounded natural to our ears.

A day later Smudge was brought home from the vet's and as his Carrier's door opened, he darted away obviously delighted to be released from his confinement. I was afraid he might not forgive us and never return but again I was wrong, for at dinnertime our docile Smudge showed up as usual. We did not want anyone in our neighbourhood to mistake our Smudge for another "dirty stray cat" and informed all our neighbours that this outdoor cat was our responsibility: neutered and inoculated, he was our "clean" pet!

For the winter of 1997-98, we hoped to make Smudge an "indoor" cat. Since he loved food, coaxing him indoors with food would be the ideal initiation. Beginning in the fall, he was fed just inside the open patio doors keeping them that way while he ate. Slowly his dish was moved further indoors and eventually into the kitchen where he ate with his sisters Nutmeg and Flash Gray-Spot. His two sisters were apprehensive about his proximity to their own food bowls but eventually all was sorted. Three cats were fed in the kitchen while Solomon continued to eat in his private dining salon.

Once, after breakfast, instead of immediately heading towards the backdoor to go outside, Smudge became curious about the rest of our home and decided to investigate the basement. Cautiously he went downstairs and discovered a furnished room at the back of our basement. After having inspected that room, for a reason unfathomable to me, he became afraid to retrace his route. Terrified, he started howling. At this stage, not being accustomed to frequent handling, picking him up bodily was out of the question. Thinking fast, I opened a can of soft food and holding it in front of his nose; he followed it greedily away from his entrapment and outside once more. Of course, I gave him a treat.

Although Smudge ate inside our home, he lived outside. Old WhiteBelly, now being the "numero uno" male in this territory, did not tolerate any other male including Smudge. We often observed Old WhiteBelly's aggressive behaviour towards Smudge who remained docile and non-territorial especially now that he was neutered. Poor Smudgy was always on the losing side and ran away, if he could. He could not one evening in November 1997 when we heard the familiar screams of a cat fight. Running outside we discovered that Smudge had been attacked in earnest this time by Old White Belly. Blood was dripping from the base of his tail.

Seeking refuge, a very frightened Smudge came indoors at George's coaxing and immediately jumped onto a small couch, in our back room, where he slept for a very long time. Even his sisters recognized something serious had happened because they did not harass him as they usually did. He remained indoors; his confidence was shattered and his behaviour remained very low-key. Only after two days, his poor wounded tail "perked up" together with his confidence.

After his two day recovery period indoors, a new habit developed. Smudge came inside every night during the remaining winter months until March. As soon as warmer temperatures arrived, it was the great outdoors for him again. The best of both worlds, Smudge became an "indoor-winter/outdoor-summer" cat.

The more comfortable he became indoors, the more he enjoyed being handled. During feeding time, a routine developed which was that he ate only after we had ruffled his fur. I guess his "ruffle-duffle" gave him the assurance he needed to "eat" amongst his sisters who continually begrudged his presence. Smudge purred loudly when brushed or stroked. Eventually, we could give him a "half-cuddle" by lifting only his front end off the floor. His hind feet had to remain firmly planted on the floor otherwise anxious struggling followed.

The annual vet visit was just such a struggle because I found that a frightened, unwilling twelve pound cat was almost unmanageable. At home, sheer determination on our part propelled him into the carrier and persistence removed him from the carrier at the vet's office. Wisely, our vet reduced Smudge's annual examination to the absolute minimum, inoculations only, because too much handling was just too stressful for everyone!

Solomon, our blue-eyed king, accepted Smudge immediately and vice-versa, Smudge acknowledged Solomon as the patriarch of the feline troupe in our home. The two became great friends with much grooming and friendly play-fighting. Smudge and Solomon often napped together on the backrest of our couch while we were seated. Occasionally, Smudge stretched out his paw to touch me in a playful gesture: naturally I responded! On one occasion he sniffed my hair and gave it a lick: the taste must have been unlike any fur he had ever groomed!

Acceptance from his sisters was a different matter, never to be resolved entirely especially since Smudge was indoors only during the coldest winter months. Every winter the indoor hierarchy between himself and his sisters had to be re-established. Smudge's behaviour towards his sisters was rather indifferent whereas his presence was grudgingly tolerated by his sisters.

Nutmeg, who was jealous of Smudge's friendship with Solomon, taunted him mercilessly. But finally, Smudge had enough and took a menacing stand in front of Nutmeg. His limbs, neck and shoulders were taut and with raised hackles and flattened ears, Smudge threatened to fight. Nutmeg, who is only used to play fighting with Solomon and several pounds lighter than Smudge, very wisely backed off immediately and left him alone after that confrontation. Flashie was also jealous but, as long as her portion of food remained abundant, she left Smudge alone except for the occasional hiss or swat. I guess that his sisters had to let him know, that they, not he, were permanent indoor residents.

Someone told us that orange cats in particular, have the most affectionate good-natured docile personalities. Certainly our experience with Smudge verified this statement who was easy-going and playful. His eyes became oh, so eloquent when he wanted to be let outside; his eyes became soft and pleading while his face puckered up so that his whiskers stood forward in an adorable manner. We've never witnessed anything as expressive in any other animal.

In the four years that he was a part of our lives, Smudge became "semi" domesticated and as described earlier, learned to enjoy a certain amount of handling. His trust eventually extended to lying beside us on a couch; even to placing head, chest and fore legs on a lap but not yet his whole body. In time, we are convinced that he would have become a true "lap cat" but his life ended horribly on April 16, 2000. Smudge was a very special cat whose unique personality remains in our memory.

We wrote the following article that was printed in our local newspaper.

"A Warning

The effects of anti-freeze poisoning on a small animal are horrible: lethargy, nausea, vomiting, with slow increasing paralysis over a two day period before death provides a release to the agony.

Normally, upon arriving home after work, our cats would come running either into the kitchen to be fed or running to the back door to be let out. Arriving home on Friday evening April 14, 2000, our one cat Smudge did not move from his spot on the couch. A truly outdoor cat who had come inside that morning, eaten an unusually small breakfast, he had chosen to remain inside that day. His lethargy was very unusual. When he finally did move, we noticed he seemed to have little control in his hind quarters; he staggered in an uneven path and vomited. He staggered a few feet away and lay down. He seemed to have no energy to move further. During the remainder of this evening, he vomited several more times and each time had less energy, at one time he lay down so that his tail lay in his own vomit.

That evening, we brought him to an Emergency Clinic where blood work etc., was done to determine the cause of his illness. Saturday at 2:00AM we were told the blood chemistry showed acute malfunction of his kidneys. At 7:00AM, we were informed he was immobile, could not even control the muscles in his mouth to keep it shut and that there was no hope. His symptoms and blood chemistry results were apparently consistent with the effects of ethylene-glycol (anti-freeze) poisoning. We were present at 7:30AM April 16, 2000 when a euthanasia dose was administered to his paralyzed little body.

Smudge had been a very healthy, affectionate, neutered orange and white male cat. Although born outside on May 14, 1996 to feral parents, we had fed him since he was eight weeks old. Eventually he would be coaxed inside for the four coldest months of every winter. As soon as the first sign of spring arrived, Smudge would remain outside only coming inside to eat, sleep when exhausted or, as in this case, when mortally ill. Smudge's needless death is heartbreaking.

Please everyone; try to keep your driveways clean from the drippings of poisonous anti-freeze."

Kit-Kat: The Seeker

A brave small cat who sat midstreet
looked for a home
in which to sleep.

She found our neighbour
whose name is Germaine
who took her in and there she'd remain.

The last of her years, four in all,
became,
the very best of all.

The best of food, warmth & affection
she finally saw
her image of Heaven.

Lately, it seemed as though Kit-Kat was always outside: early in the morning when we left for work and later when we returned home around dinnertime. Much later, just before midnight, when George had his last cigarette of the day, he observed her sitting in the middle of our quiet street. A lonely sentinel; waiting for what, or, seeking whom? Often this lonely sentinel would wander over to George for a little pat or a chat; sometimes she would follow him and try to come inside our home.

Though her long black fur kept her quite warm, March nights were still very cold, hovering around the freezing point. I often saw Kit-Kat curled up against the cement curb on the asphalt of her driveway while blustery north winds howled over her. An outside shelter for her was not visible nor a bowl of water to quench her thirst while her owners were at their daily work. We wondered if she no longer wanted to be inside her own home of seventeen years. Had she given in to ancient longings and become a nocturnal cat preferring to stay outside?

Although she sought George's company, she displayed unpredictable reactions to stroking or attempts at brushing out her matted fur. A stroke on the wrong spot provoked a flash of extended claws accompanied by a warning growl. Even a scratch under the chin was not always welcome. Perhaps she was becoming just plain cantankerous in her old age or perhaps, due to old age, she was suffering from arthritis and a sore mouth with inflamed gums and broken teeth. Whatever the reason for her contrariness, one had to tread carefully. For me, a light pat on the top of her head seemed to be the only safe place.

A strong personality with the experience of a lifetime, I have seen her hold at bay two neighbourhood dogs, one large and one small. What an amazing sight that was; her green eyes glaring, black nine pound Kit-Kat would confidently hold her ground against a Doberman Pincher or a dainty Pomeranian as they barked and ran circles round her. A lightning quick flash of claws would conclude the stand-off and an exasperated dog went home to lick his wounded pride. No doubt, each dog planning wiser strategic canine moves for their next encounter with this indomitable small feline.

As spring became early summer, Kit-Kat continued to remain out of doors as far as we could tell. In her youth, she was probably a fine hunter but at this stage of her life we had never noticed her stalking or climbing in pursuit of prey. Suspecting she was hungry, George brought some food outside; Kit-Kat ate greedily, just like one of our many neighbourhood strays.

After George's initial offering of food, Kit-Kat came over more frequently and that caused much consternation amongst our own cats which are mightily possessive about their larder. After all, this is their property! Nevertheless, mature determined lady that she was; Kit-Kat did what she wanted, when she wanted. Begrudgingly our cats left a large space around her while she waited near our side entrance. As we did not want to encourage any feline fights, we stopped feeding Kit-Kat.

Kit-Kat then visited our neighbour Germaine who had known her since she was a kitten. Like us, Germaine too wondered what Kit-Kat's "home" situation was all about. Realizing this elderly feline was hungry, Germaine offered regular feedings. Shortly thereafter, we observed Kit-Kat spending most of her days and nights around our neighbour's home; gratefully accepting every delicious morsel that was offered. In between meals, Kit-Kat snoozed on the front steps, being warmed by the late afternoon sun, or, in the shelter of the car-port on rainy days. Staying close to her new larder, George never again saw her sitting in the middle of our street late at night. By the end of the summer, we rarely saw Kit-Kat in the vicinity of her original home.

While being fed outside one morning late in the fall, Kit-Kat scurried by Germaine's legs, through the open door, inside her home and downstairs into the basement. Before Germaine could catch her, Kit-Kat had climbed onto a comfortably upholstered chair and, as if she belonged, curled up and fallen asleep instantly. Our neighbour, softy and kindred cat lover that she is did not have the heart to put elderly Kit-Kat outside again. As George had always suspected, our lonely sentinel had, at last, found the home for which she had diligently sought.

Though they must have been aware, Kit-Kat's original owners never inquired after her; perhaps the move was one of mutual consensus. For the next four years, Kit-Kat lived in her new home being properly cared for until the infirmities of extreme old age finally caught up with her. Having lost her hearing, vision and control over bodily functions, she was kindly put to sleep. As she surely deserved, Kit-Kat, The Seeker received total care, love and affection at the end of her twenty-one years.

Scruffy

a.k.a "Old White Belly"

Scruffy,
Oh, Scruffy,
what have we done?

One more life
you felt was won
but then there was none.

Scruffy,
Oh Scruffy,
what have we done?

As of July 26, 2001 Scruffy, our resident stray gladiator, is fighting battles in feline Elysian Fields. And what a gladiator he was! A terror to other younger inexperienced male cats, he reigned supreme for four years disposing of rival males without mercy. During these years, he was Cinnamon's champion and sire to her litters. Scruffy and his queen were a devoted pair through hot summers and very cold winters but constant battles in her honour left his body covered in a mass of scars. The story of this gladiator, in my opinion, perhaps like that of all gladiators, is poignant but not glorious.

Visually, Scruffy was no longer an attractive cat but one as implied by his name. His ruff was thick with scar tissue; a large part of one ear and a small portion of his right upper lip were missing. The under belly and legs were a lacklustre white while the shoulders and back were a mottled tan-yellow-black colouring: all of it unkempt in appearance. A thin scrawny beringed tail looked more like an excuse rather than a proud plume. Overall, not an attractive tomcat; looking after his territory, queen and offspring required all his energy leaving none for the usual meticulous grooming that one expects of cats. I had named him "Old White Belly" in 1996 when he first made his appearance.

He considered our property his territory and continually challenged or attacked our three cats to the point where they were fearful of venturing into their backyard! His aggressive nature might be normal for an unaltered male however we wanted our own cats to feel comfortable outside on our property and chased Old White Belly away at every opportunity. Naturally, I was not entirely successful at keeping him away and often saw him "marking" our property as his territory.

In early August 2000, when he reappeared, after an absence of about three weeks, I was shocked at his appearance; he seemed to be at death's door. Painfully dragging one hind leg and moving very slowly, he was literally skin and bones. His condition was likely the result of a fight or possibly an accident but who would ever know? Even though I did not like him, his dreadful condition overcame my antipathy. I ran out to the driveway with food and water for him. Poor creature, voiced his appreciation to us for food and water placed in front of him. That first feeding was the beginning of our close association with Old White Belly.

Now that I was resolved to help him regain his health, I felt that "Old White Belly" was too long and awkward and renamed him "Scruffy" which seemed more appropriate and endearing. Due to his poor condition, I fed him extra vitamins as well as fresh frozen raw cat food available in certain pet food stores. He slowly became stronger and eventually was observed to spend a few seconds grooming himself: his untended white fur appeared a little brighter. With regular feedings, Scruffy's health continued to improve.

We had fed him in our driveway but this was awkward for us. We intended to feed him outside on our patio and began moving his food bowl in that direction. Of course, he knew I came through the patio doors with his food and before long he was sitting there waiting. One day, when either I was late or he particularly hungry, he walked through the door I had opened and, as though he owned the place, into the kitchen passing our trio in the hall. Our cats looked aghast at this intruder but none had the nerve to contest his presence even within their own home! In my mind I had horrendous visions of a gigantic cat fight with fur flying in all directions. Not knowing if he would allow me to pick him up, I lured him outside again with his food bowl. On many occasions, I have discovered that food is always a great incentive!

Twice daily, Scruffy waited patiently for his meals outside the patio door. Simultaneously, inside the patio door was our own tribe waiting patiently to go outside. Once that door was opened, there was a momentary awkward impasse between Scruffy and our trio before it passed and resolved itself with some swatting, hissing and spitting. Now that we fed Scruffy, we observed a slight change in the relationship between him and our trio. Whereas previously Scruffy attacked without hesitation, he now tolerated our pets and they begrudgingly tolerated him.

Even though I was willing to feed him, I remained reluctant to touch him. George, being more compassionate, decided to do something about his ungroomed state and took an extra brush outside one day. Scruffy did not run when the brush touched his fur; on the contrary he leaned into the brush and began to purr and drool! George was surprised to discover that not only did Scruffy love to be brushed but he also loved being handled. Eventually, whenever George came outside, Scruffy came running and climbed onto George's lap for a grooming session or a nap; preferably both, thank you! Sometimes I saw the two of them napping together in the warm afternoon sun on the patio. It was obvious to me that a special relationship had developed between these two males!

For the cold winter ahead, George once more, softy that he is, constructed a house for Scruffy from our old wooden composter. It was covered with plastic sheeting on the outside and inside, completely lined with insulation. The slanted lid of the composter was shingled like any good roof. A construction heat lamp kept the inside above freezing. Not only was it waterproof and heated, it was also vented, via a moveable slot of wood. A raised platform inside was big enough to accommodate Scruffy's queen, Cinnamon, as well. Once ready for occupancy, George carefully chose a spot to place this cat house beside our hedge separating our yard from that of our neighbour. The hedge was overgrown and provided excellent protection against drifting snow. The cat house opening faced south away from the prevailing northern winds.

We also made a feeding station out of Styrofoam on the back deck, close to the patio door, where Scruffy would be protected against wintry elements while eating. Deep in winter's snow, there was a well-worn pathway of kitty tracks between the feeding station on our patio and the heated cat-house approximately fifteen feet away.

Of course, with his health regained, territorial fights resumed as well. Early in 2001, we noticed the frequent presence of a long-haired black cat. The two were seen stalking each other with the inevitable result of regular fights. Scruffy suffered terrible bloody wounds on his neck and particularly his left front leg. Twice, large dreadful abscesses developed on his lower spine near the base of his tail. Miraculously, within a week or so this awful looking wound, with a one inch diameter, healed as dead skin fell away. The wound closed and new fur would grow but, just as one wound was healed, another one was inflicted; a vicious cycle.

Cinnamon gave birth to another litter in early 2001 but only two weeks later she behaved as though in heat again.

Surely this was impossible if she was still feeding her litter? As the weeks went by we no longer saw any activity near the cat-house nor did we ever see her kittens. We wondered what had happened. George decided to look inside the cat house and discovered a dead kitten. It was perhaps only a few weeks old; without visible wounds, we can only assume it died of starvation. Why had Cinnamon abandoned her kitten? Was Scruffy no longer able to protect his offspring from another male? Who knows what tragedy had unfolded there. Nature is not compassionate, it is brutal.

Although Scruffy had reigned supreme for the last four years, he had been around for many more years and I suspect he might now be about ten years old. No longer in his prime, he now lost battles. How much longer could his battered body recover from regularly inflicted ghastly wounds? We wondered whether the fighting would cease if he were neutered and were told that the urge to fight remains strong for about six weeks; in fact it may never disappear completely. Whether neutered or not, Scruffy's rival would continue attacking until either Scruffy died or disappeared from this territory. The new male would then replace Scruffy as Cinnamon's champion. An age-old battle about survival of the fittest.

If neutered, could we bring him inside? Considering this option, we foresaw many obstacles, the least of which was that as an outdoor cat of many years, he likely wouldn't adapt to becoming an indoor cat. We know from experience with Solomon, that neutering does not stop a male from spraying. If Scruffy had to share indoor territory with Solomon, would one or both feel compelled to spray inside our home to "mark" their respective territories? To bring the old gladiator inside would not be fair to our own trio, especially Solomon, whose patriarchal standing with Nutmeg and Flash Gray-Spot, would likely be usurped by the older Scruffy. Our King Solomon dethroned; no, we could not let that happen! Reluctantly, we concluded that bringing Scruffy inside our home was not a viable option.

What then could we do? Since we found him affectionate and easy to handle, we believed he was not a feral cat but one that had been abandoned. When another abscess was festering, we decided to take him to a humane shelter. Hoping that a kind soul would adopt him if his story was known, we gave the information to the receptionist who seemed compassionate. She told us the doctor would examine Scruffy and we could telephone for an update in a few days. Believing the "right thing" had been done for our ageing gladiator and with optimism in our hearts, we went home.

Two days later on July 27th I called and was told Scruffy had been euthanized on July 26, 2001. Apparently he had been a very sick cat. Such unexpected news was devastating and yet, in retrospect, we should have realized that valuable tax dollars wouldn't be spent on an old battle-scarred sick cat. Even if Scruffy's wounds had been treated and healed, he would not have been a prime candidate for adoption. Most likely, he would have languished in a cage and eventually been euthanized. There are so many cats needing homes and it's my belief that only a few attractive healthy ones are lucky.

Our hope that Scruffy live a few more years in comfort and protection was very naive. We had cruelly betrayed the trust that he had given us willingly and live with the consequence of our action. Should we ever have to face a similar situation, we must choose a different approach.

An Introduction to Three Yarns

"Robert Summers, my friend and kindred cat lover, suggested I write a short story from the feline perspective. His idea gave birth to not one, but three tales, entitled: Mariah, Mathew, and Lotte: My Devovted Homo Sapien. The first two names belong to Robert's charming cats who, I realised, were eager to tell their stories. Equally keen was my own Solomon whose efforts created the third fable. My heartfelt thanks to you, Robert!"

----- Charlotte Miller

Mariah

On our planet earth, there are millions of cats and of those, untold numbers are tabbies but of all the tabbies, there was only one Mariah; Mariah Summers.

Last Saturday, August 21st 2004, having reached the age of fifteen, Mariah succumbed to the infirmities of such a grand age and was released from her current life to rejoin her many tabby sisters in the majestic constellation "Leo". There, as the newcomer, she enthralled a huge audience in the Hall of Wisdom with the tale of her life on the planet earth.

Mariah began her tale simply, by explaining that she and her siblings were born many years ago, in a barn on the outskirts of the city Toronto. Though her mother was a wanderer, she was a good mother and as such, she had found a warm, dry barn in which to give birth to a large litter. Like a snippet of a dream, most of those early days are now only a vague memory but Mariah did remember people coming into the barn to observe her with her siblings; those people stood, "ooohed and aawwed" and then disappeared. Two moons later when she and her siblings were running helter-skelter outside the barn, playing with each other as well as chasing birds and butterflies, some of these people returned and one by one her sisters and brothers disappeared. Mariah was mystified but clever enough to connect her siblings' disappearance to people. Naturally she became wary of people but that would change completely in a short time.

When first observed, Mariah's gambolling antics and striking coat with light green eyes had won the heart of a handsome, dark-haired young man named Robert Summers. He had made it his goal to take care of and protect her and so at eight weeks of age, Robert became Mariah's caregiver.

Upon reaching her new home, she discovered that Robert had a surprise waiting for her and that was Robert's resident cat named Mathew, a strapping, healthy orange tabby. Mathew was then nine years of age and immediately took it upon himself to teach young Mariah everything he had already learned about life. He became her lifelong companion and partner in play. They were a handsome feline pair: she, a dark striped tabby with citrine coloured eyes and he, ginger coloured except for a white muzzle below amber coloured eyes. Rivalry never reared its ugly head between this devoted pair; Robert had chosen well.

Such fun she and Mathew had, chasing each other and climbing over and under furniture, not to mention all the toys Robert brought home. Mariah tells her audience, "It was wonderful; I could not have been luckier! The only sad thing in my life was that Robert left every morning, stayed away during daylight and returned at dusk. Mathew and I had no idea what that meant." She continued her tale with, "Then there was a move to another home and that was exciting because not only was it larger with more nooks and crannies to explore but there was a second caregiver named James who stayed with us all the time. During evening hours we had not one but two caregivers. Oh yes, Mathew and I were very lucky indeed!"

There was a third move and this one Mariah considered the best of all. She loved the view from their latest home high above the tree line. The unique vantage point from a favourite perch on the back of a soft couch was higher than she could possibly ever have climbed herself; an infinite panorama paraded daily before her eyes. As she took in that breathtaking view, she often reflected on what her life might have been without Mathew, Robert and James. Life in a barn, as a mouser might have been "natural" but one filled with risks of exposure not only to the four seasons but from predatory creatures much larger than she could have handled. As a Lady of Leisure who is waited upon, hand and foot, she blinked contentedly in appreciation with her luxurious surroundings.

"So lucky," she mused, not a barn cat scorned but a beloved condo-cat.

At fifteen years of age, Mariah continued to enjoy the occasional bit of play but Mathew cannot participate because he, at twenty-four years of age, is nearly blind and completely deaf. She remembered Mathew's protectiveness when she first entered his life as an eight week old kitten and realized that it's now her role to protect and guide him. Acting as his ears and eyes, Mathew confidently follows her telepathy and scent around their home. Still, as a reminder of their youthful exuberance, Mariah tries to engage Mathew into a token boxing match after their evening meal but the effort is too exhausting and instead Mathew sought a spot to rest. She reluctantly accepted that her lifelong friend dreamt more and more about events long ago. Mariah remained loyally at her ageing companion's side.

Mariah too, had slowed considerably though people and objects still piqued her interest. Like all female creatures, she was the more vocal of the two and enjoyed greeting and exchanging a tad of gossip with the numerous cat lovers who entered her home. Recently, Mariah told her rapt audience, she felt unwell; wobbly on her feet, weak and very little appetite. Most embarrassing for the fastidious Mariah, she could not find the strength to reach her litter box. "Can anyone here imagine?" she asked. "Awful, simply awful!" her audience commiserated. Lately, during the dark of night, she felt more drawn than ever before to her favourite constellation "Leo" and thought more frequently about her brothers and sisters: she was tired, so very tired. A visit to the doctor confirmed that her frail body could no longer cope. With great compassion in their hearts, her caregivers, Robert and James, reluctantly released Mariah.

At the conclusion of her story, a dignified Mariah states "I am happy to be amongst all of you once again: to be free of discomfort and pain but I greatly miss my life's companions." Wise Elders seated amongst the audience in the Hall of Wisdom were enchanted with Mariah's tale and delighted to hear that she had been treated with so much love and kindness. They knew, only tabbies with positive experiences will wish to be reborn and live another life elsewhere on earth. Looking forward to another life, Mariah knows that Mathew will eventually transcend and hopes he will join her to relive all their adventures once more. She cannot imagine life without Mathew.

Mathew

Prior to Mariah's disappearance, Mathew still enjoyed life, though at a stately pace. Two years ago during his twenty-third year, Mathew's world became silent. Sounds were no longer heard and could not aid him during his daily routine. Also, through a haze of dimmed vision, he walked carefully in his silent world in search of familiar warm hands, favourite spots, the litter box or his food bowl. Night lights were installed for his benefit. He relied upon his memory and scent, both faculties remained strong, to guide him to the destination of his choice.

Scent drew Mathew to the food bowl which was filled twice daily with delectable morsels: he wished he would have received more but did not. Why not, he wondered and conveniently forgot that his heavier weight caused him difficulties with climbing, walking and grooming. Nevertheless, he dreamt of a never-empty food bowl and wandered over to check several times each day, just in case!

But it was Mariah, his companion of fifteen years, who was there to help him find his way. He could not envision life without her. He knew she was not well but when Mariah passed away suddenly last fall, Mathew knew the sunset of his life had arrived. His world tumbled yet again, when Robert was hospitalized. Mathew could not cope with such devastation and sought comfort in James' company, night and day. To Mathew's joy, Robert returned one week later. Mathew fervently hoped that through some miracle Mariah might also return but as the days passed, he knew that his was a futile hope.

Life without his lithe and graceful, green-eyed Mariah felt hollow. She was the one who "heard" for him. Without her scent to follow, he found it difficult to find familiar pathways around his home. Gone also, were the after-dinner boxing matches during which, gentleman that he was, he always let her win. Without hearing and minimal sight, he concentrated on events of long ago. The memories of his remarkably long life are numerous and returned often to fill his current days with comfort, light and pleasure.

Oh, those days of his early youth when he could run like the wind and climb like a vine, the frequent games Robert played with him in their different homes are so vivid as if they occurred only a moment ago. He remembered his very first home where Robert lived with his family. It was a busy home with many family visits but it was also one filled with overwhelming sadness when Mrs. Summers became mortally ill. Mathew remembered keeping vigil in the doorway of her room where he remained, providing his comfort, until her demise. Mathew adored Mrs. Summers.

Not long afterwards, Robert moved into his own home, a high rise apartment and what a view that offered! High above the tree-line, it offered miles and miles of open view but far below, he saw Robert walking across the road to enter another building each morning; Mathew realized he would be alone until Robert returned at dusk. Mathew was a very sociable feline and loved company but in Robert's apartment there was none. He felt alone and was lonely.

During Indi's ninth year, Robert brought home a young female kitten. She was named Mariah. Mathew became the object of Mariah's instant hero worship. As for Mathew; well, who could resist and not respond to the adoration Mariah bestowed? Mathew certainly could not! It was not long before she joined him during his daily running and climbing expeditions. She filled his days with companionship especially during Robert's absence. So much fun they had! Much later in life, those youthful exuberant times were relived through daily two-punch boxing matches just after their evening meal at 7:30 PM. Mariah's presence completed Mathew's life.

After another move, James entered their lives. Mathew and Mariah were delighted to discover that while Robert left home each day, James remained at home; a soothing voice for their sensitive hearing and gentle hands to groom and caress their fur. James' lap was always available for warmth and comfort during nap time. Robert and James are avid collectors of beautiful ornaments and while Mathew and Mariah wanted to play with these ornaments, they knew that was forbidden. Instead they were satisfied to gaze quizzically at the sparkling reflections thrown by these ornaments and as those reflections bounced off walls, Mathew and Mariah were delighted to chase those illusive playful lights.

Mathew never felt the touch of an unkind hand nor heard harsh words enter his ears; as a result he became a trusting and loving cat. Full of goodwill, he approached all who entered his home. Guests in turn could not help but be charmed by amber-eyed, ginger coloured Mathew especially when he nestled against them on the couch. His pure white muzzle was then arched to receive the longed-for chin scratch that could not be denied. Mathew's appreciation was expressed through eyes closed in blissful gratitude and accompanied by an audible purr that emanated from the depth of his heart.

Since Mariah's passing, his home felt strangely silent. Though Robert and James tried their best to fill the void, Mathew felt lonely and longed for Mariah's company. And as his longing grew, his interest in daily living diminished. Mathew's frame weakened as his interest in food disappeared. Though he drank to quench his thirst, his body did not absorb the necessary fluids and his thirst increased. Mathew could not find, or forgot, the location of familiar spots. He became disoriented; it was all too tiring. He was exhausted yet sleep no longer refreshed. One afternoon, as he rested on Robert's lap, twenty-five year old Mathew "looked" pleadingly at Robert in that unique way felines do when they wish to be released. Robert understood immediately. With great reluctance and sorrow, Robert and James responded to Mathew's request. On

May 3, 2005, Indi was mercifully released from his earthly life.

A New Cycle Begins

Mathew awoke from an unusually deep and restful sleep and realized he felt vibrant and strong as he had in his prime. More importantly, his sight and hearing were as sharp as in his youth. He gazed around in wonder because nothing seemed familiar, yet he felt not threatened but comforted. The meadows looked fresh and green with a magnificent cloudless blue sky up high. Circling above him were birds in brilliant plumage while on the ground all familiar ground dwellers roamed, though his natural instinct to hunt any of these creatures, inexplicably, did not rise. What a strange and wondrous place this is, he thought. Where am I? Could this be the constellation of Leo, he wondered? If true, then Mariah will be here!

Off in the distance, his sharp eyes saw a familiar feline form approaching with the same lithesome, graceful spring that he remembered so well from his youth. Yes! His beloved Mariah was racing to meet him. Mathew's joy was complete. Mariah's joy was equally great because she had waited patiently for her life's companion to join her. She escorted Mathew to the Hall of Wisdom, where she had held the audience captive with her story not too long ago. Again, the great hall was filled to capacity in order to welcome Mathew into Leo's constellation. The wise elders were eagerly anticipating a tale as heart-warming as Mariah's.

With Mariah by his side, Mathew felt ready to tell the story of his earthly life and as a hush came over the crowd, he began, "Greetings everyone. My name is Mathew Summers and I lived on the planet earth for a quarter of a century." He heard gasps of awe. "Oh, how wonderful!" and "So lucky!" he heard their whispers. "Yes, mine was a very long and happy life and that longevity is a testament to the love and protection

I received from my devoted caregivers, Robert Summers and
James Dryden…"

Lotte: My Devoted Homo Sapien

My Himalayan Hound;
a breed unheard of you say
but I assure you such a one exists
for he and I are close friends.

My Himalayan Hound,
is playful and mischievous
with ice-blue eyes he resembles
a pale Lilliputian mammoth.

Harnessed, he leads me around our garden
and marks particular spots.
Indoors, while standing on my shoulder,
he licks my hair or rests on my feet.

My Himalayan Hound,
like any other follows me everywhere.
He loves to jump for a toy thrown high.
Solomon; devoted and unique.

Never in front, always behind
Solomon pads quietly to his food bowl.
Discreet, patient, loyal and polite is
my Himalayan Hound.

Though feline, I consider myself a hound; a Himalayan Hound to be precise. Unlike many of my brother felines, who only tolerate their Homo sapien caregivers, I am truly fond of mine. Others of her own kind call her Charlotte or Lotte for short but I have special ways to attract her attention and, Lotte, clever lady, has learned to respond. When I blink at her in greeting, she blinks in return! She reacts to my telepathy though somewhat slowly because her perception is naturally not as refined. To communicate with me, she has chosen to call me Solomon. Naturally, to please her, I respond whenever she calls "Solomon?"

That is, of course, if that moment is suitable and I am not occupied with one of the many daily chores requiring my complete concentration. For instance, first and foremost, I must know which other uninvited tomcats have been in my territory? Which feathered friends have visited my yard today? How many pesky squirrels have traversed Hydro Lane # 409 today? Secondly and only slightly less important, where and what are the other felines under my care up to; do they require my assistance or experience to solve a problem? Is my presence required to provide amusement or a game thereby alleviating their boredom? Last but not least, the prodigious grooming of my luxurious fur cannot always be interrupted at Lotte's whim but she cannot be expected to know when I am preoccupied by any of these weighty matters. I attend her call, if convenient, simply because she is an extraordinarily dear caregiver.

Ours was a match foretold by our Himalayan Grand Master and described in our Book of Wisdom long, long ago before the time of Homo sapiens. I understand that currently Homo sapiens believe that our elegant breed was recognized only a few decades ago; what nonsense! Ours has been around for untold centuries. Wise Himalayans roamed our beloved mountain range which was covered with lush forests and filled with exotic feathered birds; a time when flying fish skimmed over our mountainous streams. Only when the world cooled did our terrain change and slowly our bodies adapted; our legs grew shorter as did our ears; nature's answer to retaining maximum body heat. Our fur grew dense and longer, our eyes bluer to withstand the eternal glare of snow and ice. Our feet grew wider, the better to run over our Himalayan Mountains now covered year round with deep snow. As food slowly dwindled, our species almost became extinct. Only the wisest and hardiest of our breed survived. Such is the stuff of which my ancestors were made!

I have much more to tell about my illustrious ancestry, but that is another longer tale. After all, this story is not about me but "Lotte; My Devoted Homo sapien".

At eight weeks of age I was ready to leave my litter mates, a little reluctantly I will admit but then I knew I was destined for life in a city greater and mightier than Bobcaygeon. Please do not misunderstand me because there is nothing wrong with Bobcaygeon but my breeding community consisted of many felines of all classes, plus there were horses and dogs; none of whom came from pedigreed backgrounds, I can assure you! My continued presence in such surroundings would simply not do justice to my ancient lineage. My destination was the huge metropolis of Toronto, the home of my Homo sapien caretaker.

On the appointed day, Lotte and her family arrived in their rumbling metal wagon to transport me to Toronto. My, oh my, what a long miserable journey that was and so noisy. I am not too proud to tell the reader that I was frightened and crawled up Lotte's arms and around her neck to see where all the noise originated. Thousands of similar metal wagons rode beside us in the same direction or passed us by with even greater speed. I noticed that while we went in one direction, other wagons far away went in the opposite direction. There was so much to see that every so often my eyes needed rest. I climbed down her arms and rested in her lap but only for a minute or so because my innate curiosity got the better of me, so back up I crawled. Her soft arms were the perfect venue for, and frequently used by, my delicate young claws.

I am certain that none of my ancestors ever observed all that I saw on that day and, as the present Custodian of our Book of Wisdom, shall record my experiences with great accuracy in our hallowed document.

At long last we arrived in Toronto and the den where Lotte and her mate-for-life, George, live. Our kind does not understand such monogamy; indeed the long-held motto of my ancestors is "Live and Love" but I believe that every living creature is entitled to its own habits, even if I consider them peculiar. Actually, our kind finds all Homo sapiens a little peculiar and grossly tall especially since they only use two of their four limbs for walking. Why only two, when in fact they all have four perfectly functional limbs, is a puzzle to which my kind has yet to find an answer. After a fall to the ground, we find it quite amusing to observe them scrambling to their upright position again. Yes; they are known to fall! If it's so awkward to get up from the ground, why not stay low and use all four, I keep asking myself? But, in truth, I find their antics endearing and lovable. In any case, regarding my Toronto den, it is a little cavernous for my tastes but nonetheless cozy with many nooks and crannies wherein I can quietly contemplate the meaning of life or spend undisturbed hours of sleep.

Through my keen powers of telepathy I realized that Lotte had led a sadly neglected life during her earlier years, having been deprived of the joy our kind bestows. My goal therefore became to provide her with as much daily amusement as possible thus filling the void of her earlier years. Granted, upon entering my new den, I discovered a resident older feline who was rescued from near-death by Lotte and George. They named this cat Princess. She was blind and although Princess had wisdom of the ages, those years had not mellowed her personality. What a cantankerous grouch! No matter how I played, postured or communicated, Princess would have nothing to do with me. All the knowledge and inherent wisdom of my lineage could not break her motto of "Leave Me Alone!"

Her motto and likely that of her ancestors, was a pole away from mine and maybe, just maybe that is the key to her personality. If her ancestors had the same short fur and thin long legs with narrow feet as Princess, they probably suffered miserably through the cold ages of long ago. Why, it's a miracle her breed survived at all but it seems to me that their personality was frozen in time and remains unthawed. A sage she might be, but not a benevolent one! Princess is not a name I would have given but then that is just another example of Lotte's and George's compassion. Exactly what joy Princess brought into their lives was inexplicable to me. Since I cannot change what is, I decided that henceforth I would concentrate fully on my goal. My Homo sapiens would soon see that I am much more entertaining.

I began my entertainment in the classic style. That is, by swinging from one sheer curtain to another to demonstrate my fine acrobatic skills. Their sheers were lovely billowing clouds and just made for this activity. Immediately afterwards, I climbed to the top of an indoor tree just to demonstrate my trapeze capabilities. As I was grandly perched on the uppermost branch surveying my new domain, the tree inexplicably fell on its side. It crashed to the floor, breaking a few ornaments standing on a small table nearby before landing on the ground. What a silly, useless tree! It lacks both normal scent and texture but Lotte seems delighted with this peculiar tree and even spends hours cleaning its leaves. Who has ever heard of cleaning trees! Sometimes, dear reader, Lotte spends time on the most peculiar activities but as I always say; "Live and Love."

One day Smudge and I devised the best game ever. I'll explain later about Smudge but first I must tell you about our game. We chased and fought with the bubbles in their waterbed! Well, we pricked each and every one of those bubbles and suddenly we were happily splashing in small puddles of water. What great fun we had that day! We exceeded anything ever done by our ancestors and expected to be generously rewarded for our splendid entertainment; perhaps with an extra ration of tuna. And, were we? No; we were scolded! Lotte doesn't always appreciate the efforts involved to amuse her. Well, I'll just keep on inventing and enlarging my repertoire of games until the right event is found that will make her and George laugh.

And find the right game I did, although that was almost one year later. Two young lassies rescued from the street also came to live in our den. They were named Flash Gray-Spot and Nutmeg; peculiar names but there you are. I have my own names for these two females but that remains between them and me. Although they are sisters they do not look alike at all; in fact their Mother has quite a reputation amongst our feline community and that too, better remain a secret! Flash Gray-Spot was instantly attracted to the elder Princess with exactly the same results that I had encountered, "Leave me Alone!" I felt sorry for "Flashie" and would have embraced her friendship except for the fact that Nutmeg had laid total claim to mine. She followed me everywhere; in short, dear reader, she was smitten. At the age of one year I was a handsome Himalayan of perfect proportion with ice-blue eyes; who could blame Nutmeg? Though she has no pedigree whatsoever, I admit she is a cute little feline of the common striped tabby kind.

Before long, Nutmeg and I became the best of pals with the exception of her brother Smudge though he essentially remained an outdoor cat coming indoors only during the snow & ice months. During Smudge's absence, I chased Nutmeg around the den; over and under chairs, sofas, tables and beds. What fun we had and when I finally caught her we had a rollicking good tumble fight. Nutmeg always flops on the ground using all four long limbs for the attack while I, though with shorter legs but greater strength, plan carefully to find a spot for a hearty nip! Ha, Nutmeg can't get through my thick fur coat and always gives up when her mouth is full of my fur. As she runs away, I give her bum a nip; so there! At that point, I hear Lotte and George laugh and realize that, at last, my goal has been achieved.

Flashie has been a little peculiar ever since she was attacked outside years ago by a nasty Tom not once but twice.

She has never forgotten and believing any attempt of mine to play is a deadly attack, she reacts in kind. Nevertheless, I continue to playfully posture in front of her and through perseverance, I believe I am changing her attitude. Though sometimes, she swats me so hard that I retaliate just to let her know with whom she is jousting. All in all, she is a good sort but huge. Her charge is a sight to behold; nineteen pounds of long fur and muscle on the run. Seeing her this way is frightening but then I remind myself; "L'état, c'est moi!" I believe her ancestors might have been those ferocious Norwegian Forest Felines of ancient lore about which so much is written in our Book of Wisdom. None of our breed has ever actually seen or met any of those creatures. Some suggest they never existed and were but a useful myth to frighten our youngsters into obedience though I believe they are no mere myth.

Speaking of weight and size let us just discuss food bowl manners for a moment. Though I love the lassies dearly, they gobble their meals as though there were no tomorrow. Sometimes they eat so fast that all is regurgitated within the hour. "Haste makes waste" is written in our Book of Wisdom and so I chew every mouthful carefully twenty times thus savouring the flavour & texture. Because I eat at a discreet pace, communicating between mouthfuls with my meal companions, I am the last to finish and this means that the lassies are hovering around me like vultures ready to pounce. Occasionally they pounce before I have had my fill! To teach them some manners, they continue to eat in the kitchen while Lotte has provided me with my own private dining room. Now as I eat in blissful peace to my heart's content I hear two anxious vultures sniffing through the open space beneath the closed door of my dining room hoping that I will leave a few morsels for them when I come outside again. I dislike having to say it but lack of pedigree always shows, doesn't it?

Not anywhere near as rotund as her sister, Nutmeg too has grown to a rather Rubenesque eleven pounds but I, as their leader, have retained my ideal weight of ten pounds; "fighting trim" to use another expression found in our Book of Wisdom. My fitness is of the utmost importance because during the last year a new bold young Tom is on the prowl in my territory. Only late in life have I felt the need to keep my territory intact and as a result bold young Tom and I have had three encounters; the last one drew blood though not mine. Until the arrival of young bold Tom I had always managed to negotiate and avoid physical confrontation as befits my "Live and Love" motto, but that no longer seems possible. To tell the truth dear reader, at heart, I dread such encounters but with bold young Tom an ancient instinct takes over.

Though fighting trim and in my prime at eight years of age, Lotte is also concerned about these encounters. These days, she refers to me as "Solly One Fang" meant affectionately but regrettably and embarrassingly true. For protection, she has fitted me with a magic cobalt blue weapon, the magic properties of which are detailed in our Book of Wisdom but I am sworn to silence and may not divulge that secret. With pride I wear this magic weapon around my neck and chest and lead Lotte around my property. The magic spell is intact because whenever we are outside, bold young Tom is nowhere to be seen!

And now, as promised earlier, I will tell you about Smudge. Like his sisters, Nutmeg and Flash Gray-Spot, he was born outside. Only when that long cold period arrived and everything freezes over, did he come indoors. Then, a week-long struggle between the three siblings erupted at the end of which Smudge successfully asserted his dominance over his sisters and all was well until next winter. Naturally, Smudge accepted my status as the Alpha male without question; what a grand chap! We became excellent friends much to the chagrin of the sisters, especially Nutmeg. She was soooo jealous! Smudge and I spent much quality time together; playing, grooming and sleeping. In his third year, poor chap ingested something outdoors causing complete paralysis and he was taken away, never to return. I entered his name in our Book of Wisdom as an honorary member on the page devoted to all special felines who have transcended before their appointed time. I missed him terribly though mourning forever was impossible with Nutmeg and Flashie needing my guidance.

Another skill of mine that amuses Lotte is my melodious vocal range for which our breed is famous. Indeed our skill was perfected in ancient times when inter-clan communications could be heard far and wide bouncing off our ice-clad mountains. At times, when the moon was brightest, clan leaders gathered with youngsters on mountain tops and informed others about births, deaths, lost family members, battle victories, new skills learnt and new hunting grounds discovered. Today, in modern times, I understand that the Swiss are famous for their "yodelling" techniques. I say, "fish feathers and copycats!"

Two years ago I suffered from Jaundice followed by a car accident that left me with fractured and broken bones. Being sick and incapacitated forced me to reflect upon and view my life ahead differently. Now, at the mature age of eight years I appreciate my beloved Homo sapiens even more. Lotte and George have always wanted lap-cats and in times gone by, they have tried countless times to lure me upon their laps. Always, I ran away believing that only 'fraidy cats sat on laps. Now I think, why not please them? Hasn't that always been my goal? I recalled that Princess sat on their laps for hours. Was that the secret to her success? Perhaps she was much wiser than I believed. Now, when hands are outstretched, I turn around allowing myself to be placed on a lap and as warm hands caress my luxurious fur, a discreet purr of contentment begins involuntarily. Oh, my foolish callow youth!

George shares the caregivers' duties although I'm not certain whether he does so willingly because he frequently mutters "I hate cats!" Nevertheless he diligently grooms us every day and clips our nails once a month. George believes clipping nails is necessary; we disagree. We "grin and bear" this event because he is firm but gentle. Flashie loves to be groomed and purrs at the sight of a comb; well in her case George's grooming is necessary because she is so rotund, she is no longer able to groom herself! Nutmeg simply loves the attention while I, due to delicate and tender skin, occasionally tolerate being groomed.

Last but not least, I will devote time to describing my favourite Homo sapien, Lotte. On page 584 in our Book of Wisdom is a statement warning us "Do not bite the hand that feeds." Some felines may wish to do exactly that but we, never, ever would contemplate such nastiness. Lotte is far too dear. We are fed twice daily; a precise amount is allotted to my lassies but I receive an extra ration whenever requested because Lotte knows that unlike the lassies, I only eat to live. When the moon is at its zenith and I've completed a thorough prowl about my den, I often feel a tad peckish and after a few discreet calls to Lotte, she arises and gives me a small moonlight snack. I think she is sweet, don't you? Like all Homo sapiens, Lotte and George go to sleep when the moon appears. What a dreadful waste of time, asleep during the finest stalking and hunting hours! I howl at their door because I'm keen to teach her what excitement is possible during those dark hours. Inexplicably, she refuses to learn; nevertheless, I keep trying.

Always eager for her company, I wait for her patiently outside the bathroom and cannot help but howl if she takes too long. When she is reading I lie on her feet or sleep on her slippers in the bedroom. When Lotte has the occasional afternoon nap, I cuddle up beside her shoulder after determining whether her hair needs grooming or not. After she returns from a lengthy absence from my den, I cannot help but chirp and prance around her with joy, then immediately retrieve a ball for her to throw high in the air and me to catch. Otherwise, I just follow her around and that is why, though feline, I am proud to consider myself a Himalayan Hound.

Throughout the ages, our Book of Wisdom has been kept by the Himalayan that embodies the very best qualities in our lofty breed. Prior to my custodianship, our hallowed document was cared for by Kaze Kaiser Dickens. He was the most majestic feline of our breed with a strong large build and a dense coat of taupe and brown-black points. His eyes, a vivid turquoise blue, held Homo sapiens spellbound. Dickens too had received Lotte's fine care until he, like all others before him, transcended into the wondrous white clouds above our beloved mountain range. But, to whom our Book of Wisdom will pass when I eventually transcend is problematic, for who could possibly surpass my own supreme character?

In the meantime, as Custodian of our Book of Wisdom, it is my intention to enter Lotte's name on page 1003 specifically devoted to extraordinary Homo sapien caregivers. Her name, one of only a few, will be there for all future Himalayans to revere. Beside Lotte's name, I will enter George's name for in keeping with my motto, it takes two to "Live and Love."

Epilogue

Although the Himalayan Book of Wisdom is designated for members of that ancient breed, a Custodian may, by exercising discretionary powers, bestow honorary membership to other felines deemed worthy of such an honour: their names and deeds to be revered forever. Similarly, a Custodian may choose to record the names of extraordinary Homo Sapien Caregivers; their names to inspire courage and confidence in timid felines.

Solomon assumed the mantle of Custodian of the Himalayan Book of Wisdom from Kaze Kaiser Dickens whose custodianship was decisive and masterful and whose deeds are meticulously recorded on the page designated for all Custodians. So far, Solomon has exhibited a surprisingly tolerant, mature flair towards his responsibilities. With his exceptionally keen intuitiveness, Solomon became instantly aware of the moment when Mathew ascended to the constellation of Leo. Considering Mathew's longevity and loving friendship with Mariah, Solomon decided Mathew was indeed worthy of honorary Himalayan membership. His name will be added to those of Mariah, Scruffy, Kit-Kat, Smudge and Princess on the page reserved for Exceptional Felines. On the page reserved for Extraordinary Homo Sapien Caregivers, Solomon will add the names of Robert and James below that of Germaine but, naturally, heading the list are the names of George and Charlotte Miller.

While Nutmeg's and Flash Gray-Spot's intuitiveness is not quite as sharp as that of Solomon, they soon realized that Mathew had been spirited to Leo's luscious landscape. The sisters know that Leo is their own eventual destination and excitedly, anticipate a joyous extended family reunion. Though daughters of feral parents, the sisters hope that they too will be awarded Honorary Membership and their names entered into the Himalayan Book of Wisdom. Nutmeg is confident that Solomon will award her that honour but Flashie, whose relationship with Solomon may tactfully be classified as uneasy, occasionally feels a tiny niggle of doubt. However, Flashie is clever enough to realize that Solomon holds the title of custodian precisely because he possesses the virtues of benevolence, compassion and wisdom in abundance and that realization dispels her doubts, most of the time.

As felines age, the drawing power of the wonders to be discovered on Leo becomes greater. Leo's star is at its brightest during the depth of night and at that moment, indoor cats will pause to sit on window sills while outdoor cats will interrupt their chase to sit; each one gazing at and mesmerized by Leo's hypnotic beauty. Each night, their yearning for the promise of Leo's fulfilment becomes greater. They know that upon arrival, each new feline will be led to the great Hall of Wisdom and there on the podium, he or she will communicate to the audience everything that was experienced on the planet earth. Eventually, when all relationships and goodwill have been re-established and spirits are fully rejuvenated, each feline will pause and consider to which earthly continent he or she will descend and so begin another cycle of life.

"I have learned that the grieving period following a pet's demise is a long process but the heartache does eventually diminish after which pleasant and joyful memories creep to the foreground again. I can tell any prospective pet owner that our cherished pets leave us with a lifetime of beautiful memories,"

----- Charlotte Miller